CAMPAIGN 82

EDGEHILL 1642

FIRST BATTLE OF THE ENGLISH CIVIL WAR

SERIES EDITOR: LEE JOHNSON

CAMPAIGN 82

EDGEHILL 1642

FIRST BATTLE OF THE ENGLISH CIVIL WAR

WRITTEN BY
KEITH ROBERTS & JOHN TINCEY

BATTLESCENE PLATES BY
GRAHAM TURNER

First published in Great Britain in 2001 by Osprey Publishing, Elms Court,
Chapel Way, Botley, Oxford OX2 9LP United Kingdom
Email: info@ospreypublishing.com

ISBN 1 85532 991 3

Editor: Lee Johnson
Design: The Black Spot

Colour bird's-eye view illustrations by The Black Spot
Cartography by The Map Studio
Battlescene artwork by Graham Turner
Index by Alan Rutter
Originated by Grasmere Digital Imaging, Leeds, UK
Printed in China through World Print Ltd.

01 02 03 04 05   10 9 8 7 6 5 4 3 2 1

For a catalogue of all books published by Osprey Military
and Aviation please write to:

The Marketing Manager, Osprey Publishing Ltd., P.O. Box 140,
Wellingborough, Northants NN8 4ZA United Kingdom
Email: info@ospreydirect.co.uk

The Marketing Manager, Osprey Direct USA,
c/o Motorbooks International, PO Box 1,
Osceola, WI 54020-0001, United States of America
Email: info@ospreydirectusa.com

Visit Osprey at www.ospreypublishing.com

Artist's Note

Readers may care to note that the original paintings from
which the colour plates in this book were prepared are
available for private sale. All reproduction copyright
whatsoever is retained by the Publisher. All enquiries
should be addressed to:

Graham Turner, PO Box 88, Chesham,
Bucks, HP5 2SR, United Kingdom
www.studio88.co.uk

The publishers regret that they can enter into no
correspondence on this matter.

Editor's Note

In the 3D 'Bird's Eye View' Battlemaps in this volume units
are represented as follows: infantry – the taller units
represent pikemen, the shorter musketeers. The 'halved'
unit symbols (red/white, orange/white) represent cavalry –
usually harquebusiers or cuirassiers. Artillery is represented
by the triangular 'arrowhead' symbols. The circular 'dots'
represent dragoons or commanded musketeers acting as
skirmishers.

KEY TO MILITARY SYMBOLS AND LINE DRAWINGS

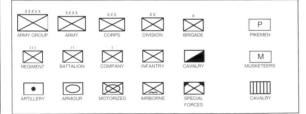

CONTENTS

ENGLAND AND WALES IN THE SUMMER OF 1642

1. London – March. The King abandons his capital to the control of Parliament.
2. York – 18 March. The King establishes his court in his northern capital.
3. Preston, Warrington, Liverpool – 20 June. Lord Strange seizes control of the Trained Band arms for the King.
4. Bridlington – 2 July. A Royalist ship *The Providence* lands two or three thousand arms, seven or eight cannon and 200 barrels of gun powder, purchased by the Queen in Holland.
5. Manchester – 15 July. Lord Strange is driven out of Manchester by armed townsmen, causing the first fatality of the Civil Wars.
6. Hull – 15–27 July. Having failed to occupy the town and seize the arms stored there, the King establishes a formal siege on 22 April but is forced to withdraw by a spirited Parliamentarian defence.
7. Kineton Heath – 30 July. Local Royalists gather to prevent Lord Brooke from moving cannon from Banbury to Warwick Castle. The Royalists later seize these cannon and use them to besiege Warwick Castle.
8. Shepton Mallet – 1 August. The Royalist Sir Ralph Hopton and the Parliamentarian William Strode MP, lead rival factions in fighting in the town.
9. Portsmouth – 2 August. George Goring, Governor of Portsmouth, declares for the King, but surrenders the

town to Parliamentarian besiegers in September.
10. Marshall's Elm – 4 August. Local Royalists defeat a party of 600 Parliamentarians.
11. Dover – 21 August. The castle is garrisoned for Parliament after a failed attempt by local Royalists to capture it for the King.
12. Worcester – The wealthy landowner the Marquis of Hereford uses his influence to make the area pro Royalist.
13. Shrewsbury – Having previously sided with local people during a trade dispute with London merchants, the King is able to use his popularity to secure the area as a sound recruiting base for the Royalist army.

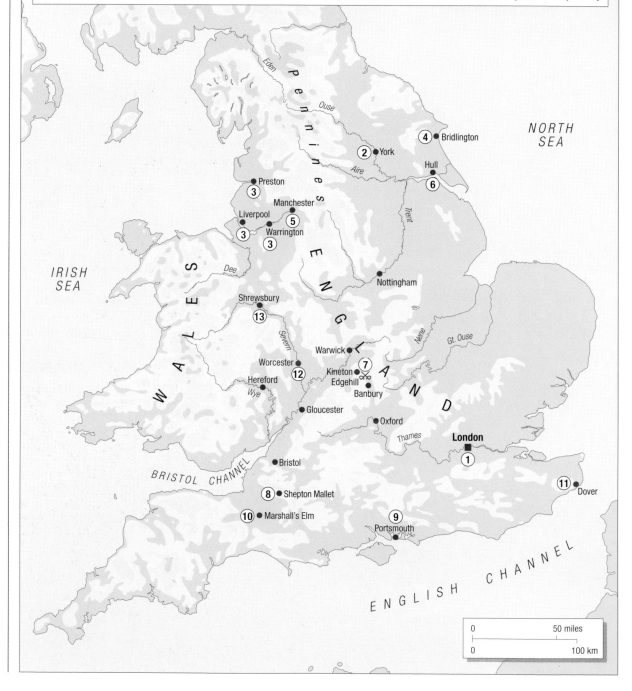

ORIGINS OF THE ENGLISH CIVIL WAR

The motto on the flag carried by a troop of Horse in the Army of Parliament read 'Religeon, King and Parliament', three competing elements which brought civil war to England.

EUROPEAN BACKGROUND

Charles I succeeded to the thrones of England, Scotland and Ireland in 1625. His reign began during a period of instability throughout western Europe, with international warfare between the major European countries as well as internal unrest. There was no single cause for the wars which were to engulf the British Isles but three themes should be considered.

Firstly, religious differences between Catholic and Protestant were becoming inextricably linked with politics and war in the Low Countries, France and the German states. Religion was not an absolute division as Catholic and Protestant states might ally against a common political opponent but religious views could create popular sympathy for fellow Protestants or fellow Catholics.

Secondly, attempts by central government to rationalise their administration at the expense of local custom and privileges caused opposition. An example of this asserting of royal authority in England was

Detail from a satirical engraving dated 1642 and entitled *Magna Britannia Divisa* by a Dutch engraver. A contemporary illustration of cavalry and musketeers. Note the trumpeter. (The British Library)

William Prynne, a Puritan pamphleteer, had his ears cut off by order of the Court of Star Chamber. Images like this one showing Archbishop Laud about to eat Prynne's ears with Bishops armed as musketeers as a guard, fuelled popular unrest.

OPPOSITE **Suckling's Roaring Boys. Sir John Suckling, a Royalist poet, courtier and gambler, was one of several officers involved in the Army plots in May 1641. This dissolute tavern rakehell image became the popular Parliament perspective on cavaliers. (The British Library)**

the imposition of 'ship money' on inland counties by the King in an effort to raise finance.

Thirdly, the value of traditional sources of income was declining in a period of rapid inflation while the expenses of government and the display of royal power were rising. Above all the costs of waging war, or simply preparing for it, were increasing as modern war required ever larger armies.

ENGLAND

The first years of King Charles's reign saw a series of unsuccessful expeditions against the Spanish and in support of French Huguenots in their rebellion against their Catholic French King. Although there was support in England for Huguenots as fellow Protestants and for any war against the Spanish, the billeting of unpaid soldiers in England and the imposition of forced loans to pay for the cost of war were highly unpopular. Charles's decision to follow a series of short-lived Parliaments with a period of personal rule between 1629 and 1640 did little to restore confidence. His marriage to the Catholic French Princess Henrietta Maria had not endeared him to English subjects who had an abiding suspicion of anything to do with the Roman Catholic faith. The introduction of elaborate forms of worship by William Laud, Archbishop of Canterbury, during the 1630s caused further dissension by offending the more Puritan amongst English Protestants, leading to accusations of 'Popish' influence.

Although these factors made Charles unpopular and created an underlying sense of unrest there was no easy channel through which opposition could be co-ordinated in the absence of regular Parliaments. The catalyst for change was the attempt by Charles and Laud to impose a new version of the English Prayer Book on the Presbyterian Church of

Suspicion of the King's intentions heightened during 1641 and an 'order was made by both Houses for disarming all the Papists in England'. Similar scenes would have occurred in 1642 as the King disarmed the local militia to provide arms for his newly raised army.

John Pym, nicknamed 'King Pym' by Royalists, was the driving force of the Parliament cause in the House of Commons.

Popish Recusants disarmed, for the greate securitr of the kingdome,

Scotland. Rioting broke out in Edinburgh and unrest swiftly spread across most of Lowland Scotland. A National Covenant was drawn up which became the basis of a national movement, an administration was formed and an army levied.

Both Charles and the Scots were able to draw upon the services of experienced officers, the former from men who had served in the Dutch Army and the latter from those who had served in the Swedish Army. However, the enthusiasm of their men was widely different. Reluctant English soldiers could not be relied upon and the First Bishops War ended when King Charles made peace after the collapse of his army's morale. Both sides realised that the war would soon resume. The King needed money for a new army and summoned the Short Parliament to obtain funds but, faced with mounting opposition in Parliament, dismissed it. His next campaign, the Second Bishops War, ended in complete disaster, his army beaten at the battle of Newburn and the Scots army invading and occupying northern England.

Forced to summon the Long Parliament to find funds to pay his army and a war indemnity which obliged him to pay for the Scots Army, Charles was now faced with a Parliamentary opposition focused around leaders such as John Pym. Officers from the poorly paid army began to meet to discuss their grievances, seeking their arrears of pay and quite possibly conspiring to march south to London to seize the city for the King and overthrow Parliament. Pym used this Army Plot to heighten fears over the King's intentions. Funds were voted to pay for the disbanding of both Scots and English armies, and the arms and military stores of the English Army were stored at Hull.

Pym was then able to use news of the King's bungled attempt to seize the head of the Scottish Covenanters in Edinburgh to persuade Parliament to call upon the London Trained Bands to provide guards at Westminster. In this atmosphere of suspicion, news reached London of an uprising in Ireland. Faced with revolt against English authority and reports of the slaughter of English and Scots settlers, it was clear that an army would be needed to suppress the rebellion. However, with the recent Army Plot in mind, there was now a strong party within Parliament that would not trust the King to appoint army officers. Their fears were heightened with news of a second Army Plot amongst officers of the garrison at Portsmouth, whose commander, Lord Goring, later emerged as a prominent Royalist. The Parliament response was to pass the Grand Remonstrance which, amongst other statements, set out their suspicion of the King's advisers and requested that he appoint no one to a senior post, military or civil, without their approval. This was not a demand the King could accept nor one upon which Parliament could negotiate.

The King's response was to attempt to impose his authority over London by placing his own supporters in key positions. He over-played his hand by attempting to seize by military force Pym and four other Parliamentary leaders. Two days later there was uproar in London amidst rumours of attack by Royalist mercenaries. Armed citizens filled the streets and the London Trained Bands mustered to defend their homes, refusing to follow orders from the Royalist Lord Mayor. The King had lost control of London and the royal family fled. The King went North to establish his Court at York while his wife took ship from Dover to buy arms in Europe.

CHRONOLOGY

WAR IN EUROPE

1562–98 French Wars of Religion.

1567–1648 Dutch Revolt in the Low Countries.

1618–48 Thirty Years War.

1648–53 Wars of the Fronde in France.

WAR IN BRITAIN

1639

First Bishops War. English at war with the Scots.

Second Bishops War. English at war with the Scots.

1641

The outbreak of rebellion in Ireland. Irish at war with the English and Scots.

1642

4 January, The King's attempt to seize five MPs in the House of Commons failed. The MPs, John Pym, John Hamden, Sir Arthur Haselrigg, Denzil Holles and William Strode, were forewarned, left the House before the King's men arrived and took refuge in the City of London.

31 January, Sir John Hotham secures Hull for the Parliament.

11 February, The Royalist Sir John Byron is replaced as Governor of the Tower of London by Sir John Conyers.

17 February, Prince Rupert lands at Dover to join King Charles.

23 February, Queen Henrietta Maria leaves England for Holland to pawn her jewellery to buy arms.

Colonel Sir Thomas Lunsford and other Royalist officers drew their swords as they quarrelled with Londoners protesting outside Westminster on 27 December 1641. The incident was a gift for Parliament propagandists.

5 March, The Militia Ordinance is passed in Parliament. An Ordinance does not require Royal Assent.

19 March, King Charles enters York.

23 April, Sir John Hotham refuses to allow the King to enter Hull.

12 June, King Charles resolves to put into execution the Commission of Array.

2–3 July, The Fleet in the Downs declares for the Parliament.

3 July, King Charles appoints his Generals, the Earl of Lindsey and Prince Rupert.

15 July, Parliament appoints the Earl of Essex to be its General.

2 August, Colonel George Goring, Governor of Portsmouth, declares for the King.

21 August, Dover Castle taken by the Parliament forces.

22 August, King Charles raises his standard at Nottingham.

7 September, Goring surrenders Portsmouth to Sir William Waller.

9 September, The Earl of Essex leaves London to join his army.

14 September, The Earl of Essex reviews his army at Northampton.

20 September, King Charles arrives at Shrewsbury.

23 September, Royalists win skirmish at Powick Bridge.

23 October, BATTLE OF EDGEHILL.

3 November, King Charles leaves Oxford to march on London.

4 November, King Charles occupies Reading.

5 November, The Earl of Essex reaches St Albans.

7 November, The Earl of Essex's army reaches London.

12 November, Prince Rupert storms Brentford, dispersing the Parliament garrison.

13 November, The Parliament army commanded by the Earl of Essex together with the London Trained Bands, commanded by Philip Skippon face the King's army at Turnham Green outside London. The King retires to Kingston.

17 November, The Earl of Essex appoints Philip Skippon, commander of the London Trained Bands to be Sergeant-Major General of the Parliament army.

3 December, The Earl of Newcastle enters York.

9 December, The King's army goes into Winter Quarters around Oxford.

13 December, Sir William Waller takes Marlborough.

20 December, The Parliament Eastern Association is formed.

27 December, Sir William Waller takes Chichester.

OPPOSING LEADERS

THE ROYALIST COMMANDERS

King Charles I (1600–1649) exercised command over all Royalist forces with the assistance of a Council of War. This Council comprised ministers, peers, generals and more junior officers whose past military experience was considered relevant. Elements of military theory were part of the education of any prince in this period and the King was also able to draw on the advice of a number of competent and experienced soldiers. However, he had no practical experience of campaigning or warfare and his inexperience, together with a tendency to follow the advice of the last man he spoke to, prevented him from exercising effective command when his generals or courtiers disagreed over strategy and tactics.

The field commander was **Robert Bertie, Earl of Lindsey** (1582–1642), with the rank of Lieutenant General of the Royalist Army. He gave up his position after the last of a number of quarrels with Prince Rupert and was mortally wounded fighting at Edgehill in command of his own regiment of Foot. Lindsey was a senior courtier whose military experience was in the Dutch school of warfare. His military career had begun under Queen Elizabeth and he had commanded English soldiers in Danish and Dutch service, been Vice Admiral and Admiral in the disastrous military adventures of the Duke of Buckingham, and governor of the garrison of Berwick in 1639 during the First Bishops War.

Patrick Ruthven, Earl of Forth (1573–1651) and initially Lieutenant General of the Horse, succeeded Lindsey. Forth was a Scottish soldier whose extensive military experience, as with so many Scots, had been in the Swedish Army. He had supported King Charles during the Second Bishops War, defending Berwick against the Scottish Army in 1640. Forth's past experience meant that he was well aware of the potential weaknesses of using Gustavus Adolphus' style of deployment with inexperienced officers and men, but with the recent quarrel between Prince Rupert and Lindsey as his example he may have thought that there was little to be gained in further debating the Prince's chosen deployment.

Royalist Horse

Prince Rupert (1619-1682), the King's nephew, commanded the cavalry at Edgehill as General of the Horse. His mother was King Charles's sister Elisabeth and his father, the Elector Palatine, a German ruler with territory along the Rhine, was the man whose acceptance of the Crown of Bohemia in 1618 sparked off the Thirty Years War in Germany. Prince Rupert, only 22 at Edgehill, had an unusually broad military experience for so young a soldier, covering the military theory of both Protestant and Catholic

Charles I, King of England, Scotland and Ireland. By 1642, he had been defeated in two wars in Scotland, there was rebellion in Ireland and civil war had broken out in England.

Robert Bertie, Earl of Lindsey, Lieutenant General of the King's Army. Lindsey gave up his commission when King Charles preferred Prince Rupert's choice of battle deployment. He was mortally wounded fighting at Edgehill in command of his regiment of Foot.

Prince Rupert, the King's nephew, depicted here as a ravening mercenary, pistol in one hand and poleaxe in the other. His poodle 'Boy' beside him.

Sir Jacob Astley, Sergeant-Major General of the King's Army. Astley was an experienced soldier who had served in the Dutch Army and as an infantry colonel during the Bishops Wars.

armies. He had served in the Dutch Army, experiencing both campaigning and siege warfare, including the internationally famous siege of Breda (1637). Captured by the Imperialists at the battle of Lemgo in 1638 while serving as a cavalry colonel in his brother's mercenary army, he was then imprisoned for three years. Prince Rupert spent much of his time in captivity studying military theory and his discussions with Imperial officers both during this period and later at the Imperial Court at Vienna introduced him to the developing military theory of the Imperial Army. By 1642, he was a competent officer with a thorough technical understanding of campaigning, siege warfare, the training methods for infantry and cavalry and various styles of contemporary battlefield deployments and tactics, and his personal charisma made him a natural leader. His weakness at this point in his career was that although he had a thorough understanding of military theory which made him one of the most technically able commanders at Edgehill, he lacked practical experience in its execution and his deployments were probably more complex than the newly raised Royalist Army could manage.

Second in command of the Royalist cavalry was **Henry Wilmot** (1613–1658), Commissary General of the Horse. Wilmot was a competent soldier whose previous experience, as with many English officers in the Civil War, included service with the Dutch Army, where he had served with Prince Rupert at the siege of Breda in 1637. In English service he had been Commissary General of the Horse in the army during the Bishops Wars. He raised a regiment of Horse at the outbreak of the Civil War and was appointed to his previous role as Commissary General of the Horse. His later career demonstrates that he was popular with the officers who served under him and several actions, notably his victory at the Battle of Roundway Down (13 July 1643), showed he was an excellent cavalry commander.

Sir John Byron (1599–1652) led Prince Rupert's second line of cavalry. Byron had some military experience in the Dutch army and had served during the Bishops Wars. He later proved to be an able, ruthless but unfortunate commander.

George, Lord Digby (1612–1677), an officer with no previous military experience and a poor understanding of his duties, led Henry Wilmot's second line of cavalry. Clarendon described Digby as 'a very gallant gentleman who had never been in action before', adding that Digby did not subsequently 'ever acknowledge that he had orders, or understood himself to be left with a reserve'.

Royalist Foot

Sir Jacob Astley (1579–1651) commanded the Royalist infantry with the rank of Sergeant-Major General. Astley was an experienced soldier who had served in the Dutch Army and as an infantry colonel during the Bishops Wars. He had been a military tutor to Prince Rupert and was a thoroughly professional and capable officer.

There is some debate over the number of brigades which made up the Royalist Army at Edgehill. Of the five known brigade commanders four, **Charles Gerard** (1618–1694), **Richard Feilding** (d.1659), **Sir Nicholas Byron** (1600–1645) and **Henry Wentworth** (1594–1644), had professional military experience, mostly with the Dutch Army. The fifth, **John Belasyse**, had no previous military experience.

15

Royalist Dragoons

Sir Arthur Aston (1590-1649) commanded the Dragoons with the rank of Sergeant-Major General of Dragoons. Aston was an experienced and able professional soldier whose career included service in the Polish and Swedish armies. Described as a 'testy, froward, imperious and tirannical person', Aston was an ideal choice as commander of Dragoons.

Royalist Artillery

Mountjoy Blount, **Earl of Newport** (1598–1666) held the position of Master of the Ordnance as he had since 1634. However, the actual day-to-day operation of the Ordnance Office had always been the responsibility of the Lieutenant of the Ordnance. The officer commanding the Royalist artillery at Edgehill was **Sir John Heydon** (d.1653), who had been Lieutenant of the Ordnance during the Bishops Wars.

PARLIAMENT'S COMMANDERS

Robert Devereux (1591–1646), Third **Earl of Essex**, commanded the Parliament Army with the rank of Captaine General. The popular second Earl of Essex (1566–1601) had been executed when his attempted rebellion against Queen Elizabeth had failed, and this made his son a focus for popular dissatisfaction against Charles I. Essex's military experience was limited, but he had served in the Dutch Army in 1624, at the same time as the Royalist General the Earl of Lindsay and as Vice Admiral to the Duke of Buckingham in the latter's unsuccessful expedition to Cadiz in 1625. Essex maintained an interest in military developments in Europe and his service as Lieutenant General of Foot in the First Bishops War had shown him to be a commander who could identify opportunities and keep his nerve. He was not appointed to any command during the Second Bishops War. Essex's military reputation has suffered unfairly in recent accounts but any assessment of his battlefield deployments against contemporary practice shows he was a competent commander and either he, or his advisers, were well aware of the latest military styles.

Parliament's Horse

William Russell (1613–1700), **Earl of Bedford**, was General of the Horse. He owed his position to his aristocratic rank not his ability. Personally brave, he had no previous military experience and was not competent to hold this position. Clarendon commented that 'the earl of Bedford had the name of general of the horse, though that command principally depended upon Sir William Balfore'.

Sir William Balfour (d.1660) was Lieutenant General of the Horse. He was a Scot, a professional soldier and an experienced, skilled officer who had served in the Dutch Army.

Sir James Ramsey as Commissary General of Horse commanded the Parliament Army's left wing at Edgehill. Ramsey was a competent professional soldier who deployed his men according to the best practice of the day. As a Scot hired by Parliament and fighting for pay, he also demonstrated the essential weakness of the mercenary, he would retreat when the odds seemed against him.

Robert, Earl of Essex, Lord General of the Army of Parliament. Essex was a competent commander who had served as a Colonel in the Dutch Army and in Royal English armies.

Sir William Balfour, Lieutenant General of the Horse for the Parliament. A Scottish professional soldier who had served in the Dutch Army.

Parliament's Foot

Sir John Merrick, an officer with European experience who had commanded a regiment during the Bishops Wars, was Sergeant-Major General of Essex's army. There is no mention of him at Edgehill and he may not have been present at the battle. Following the Dutch practice, the Parliament infantry was organised in three brigades commanded by **Sir John Meldrum**, **Charles Essex** and **Thomas Ballard**, all of whom had some previous military experience.

Parliament's Artillery

Henry Mordaunt, **Earl of Peterborough**, General of the Ordnance was the nominal commander. **Philibert Emmanuel Du-Bois**, Lieutenant General of the Ordnance, was the effective commander of the artillery.

William Russell, Earl of Bedford, was General of the Horse for the Parliament. Although personally brave he was not a competent commander and effective command of Parliament's horse was exercised by Sir William Balfour. (British Library)

William Earle of Bedford, Lord Russell of Thorn-haugh, Nominated and appointed Lord Generall of the Horse imployed for the defence of the Protestant Religion, the safety of his Ma:ts person, and of the Parliament, the preseruation of the Lawes, Liberties, and Peace of the Kingdome, and protection of his Ma:ties Subiects from violence and oppression. etc.

RAISING THE ARMIES

Parliament's control of the City of London gave it several advantages: access to arms from the arsenal at the Tower of London, control over merchants producing small arms in the City and its suburbs and the ability to raise funds to pay for arms imported through the European arms market in Holland. In addition Parliament obtained arms shipped south from Hull and by donation from the armouries of the City Guilds. It was also able to divert regiments that had been raised for service in Ireland to its own army. Volunteers from London and Southwark were enrolled at the New Artillery Garden in late July and formed into regiments commanded by Denzil Holles, Sir Henry Cholmley and Sir John Merrick. Other regiments were raised from volunteers in the south-east, for example the Lord General's from Essex, John Hamden's and Thomas Ballard's from Buckinghamshire. Volunteers for the cavalry were enlisted at the Guildhall in London from June onwards where a committee allocated them to troops and appointed officers. Other troops were raised in the counties by individual officers, including Oliver Cromwell.

The refusal of the Yorkshire Trained Bands to follow the King outside the county boundaries left him with no option but to formally raise an army to support his cause. He took the first steps in June by issuing

This illustration of a drummer, fifer, ensign and pikemen, which pre-dates the Civil War, was re-used to illustrate Civil War pamphlets. (British Library)

Satirical pamphlet of 'a Roundhead and Long-head Shagpoll' printed in July 1642 while King Charles was in York. Printed for George Tomlinson, a London bookseller who specialised in political pamphlets. The illustration shows a Puritan from London leading a Cavalier from York in a halter.

Commissions of Array to named gentry in each county, authorising them to raise troops, and military commissions to individual officers to raise regiments of Horse and Foot. The King's army began to take shape at Nottingham after the King raised his standard there. The Earl of Clarendon commented that the King 'now found his numbers increased and better resolved by it; and from Yorkshire, Lincolnshire, and Staffordshire, came very good recruits of foot; so that, his cannon and munition being likewise come up from York, within twenty days his numbers began to look towards an army, and there was another air in men's faces'. His army was still weak when the King marched to Shrewsbury in September where 'some regiments of Foot were levying for his service', and it was here that sufficient numbers of troops were concentrated to form an effective army. Although he was able to recruit soldiers, the King lacked the military supplies available to the Parliamentarians and his failure to take control of Hull denied him arms his men desperately needed.

EQUIPMENT FOR HORSE, FOOT AND THE TRAIN OF ARTILLERY

The equipment for infantry, cavalry and artillery is described in more detail in Elite 25 *Soldiers of the English Civil War (1) Infantry* and Elite 27 *Soldiers of the English Civil War (2) Cavalry*.

The Horse
By 1642 there were only two types of cavalry in English service, cuirassiers and harquebusiers. There were very few cuirassiers, troopers armoured from head to knee and armed with a sword and two pistols. Individual troopers on both sides were armed to this standard but the only complete formations were three troops in the Parliament Army.

The main battle cavalry on both sides were harquebusiers, troopers whose full equipment consisted of a helmet, back and breast plates, buff coat, sword, two pistols and a carbine. Many would have fallen far short of this ideal, some using obsolete armour, others lacking armour, carbines and pistols. A Royalist cavalryman would pass muster if armed only with a sword.

Most of the Earl of Essex's cavalry were probably equipped to the model standard, although there was a shortage of carbines. The King's army had more difficulty in obtaining arms for their cavalrymen, and its troopers were not as well equipped as their Parliamentary opponents.

The Foot

Infantry were armed as either pikemen or musketeers. Since the late sixteenth century the key to victory on the battlefield had been seen as firepower, particularly infantry firepower, but close combat between opposing bodies of pike could still be decisive in a close-fought battle. It was particularly the case with inexperienced regiments where the musketeers lacked the training to make best use of their firepower. In this situation the best option was to employ courage and determination in close combat. Even when the musketeers were well trained, pikemen were essential for any body of infantry as musketeers could not survive in open country without pikemen to provide protection against attack by cavalry.

At the turn of the century the ratio had been one to one but the number of musketeers increased during the early seventeenth century. By 1642 contemporary opinion on the best combination was changing from three musketeers to two pikemen to two musketeers to one pikeman. However, this remained the intention, an aim to be achieved if sufficient equipment was available. Where it was not possible the ratio of pikemen, whose equipment could be manufactured or improvised more quickly, could be higher. Infantry deployment placed wings of musketeers on either side of a centre of pikemen.

Model infantry equipment was musket, musket-rest, bandoleer, helmet and sword for a musketeer and pike, helmet, back and breast armour with tassets (thigh defences) and sword for a pikeman.

Cuirassier armour. Superior armour gave its wearer an advantage in hand-to-hand combat. (By courtesy of the Board of Trustees, Royal Armouries)

An illustration, probably based on an earlier print. A fifer, drummer, ensign and three pikemen.

The Earl of Clarendon commented that Essex's foot were 'completely armed' at Edgehill. However, few musketeers would have worn helmets and although warrants were issued authorising the supply of pikemen's armour to some of Essex's regiments it is probable that the majority of his pikemen had only a helmet.

The Parliamentarians had to overcome some initial confusion in the Ordnance Office as a number of its officials left London to join the King, but were able to exploit effective sources of supply. In addition to Government arsenals and private donations, deliveries of equipment purchased in Europe had arrived in time to provide Essex's army with 2,231 sets of infantry armour, 5,580 pikes, 2,690 muskets and 3,956 musket-rests by early October 1642.

The equipment of the King's infantry was famously described by the Earl of Clarendon thus: 'the foot, (all but three or four hundred who marched without any weapon but a cudgel) were armed with muskets, and bags for their powder, and pikes but in the whole body there was not one pikeman had a corslet, and very few musketeers who had swords'. However this painted too black a picture as the King's army had obtained arms from voluntary donation and the seizure of Trained Band arsenals, and this would have included pikeman's armour. The King's army would have had fewer armoured pikemen than Essex's regiments and a shortage of bandoleers would have meant some of their musketeers having to carry their gunpowder either loose in bags or with individual charges in paper cartridges.

The average ratio of musketeers to pikemen for Essex's infantry regiments at Edgehill was probably three musketeers to two pikemen, although some regiments were equipped two to one and others one to one. The King had greater problems supplying his men with arms than did Essex and a reasonable estimate would be a ratio of one musketeer to one pikeman.

The Dragoons

One other type of soldier was the Dragoon, a musketeer mounted on a cheap horse. Where possible Dragoons were issued with muskets using a flintlock rather than matchlock mechanism, the disadvantages of carrying lighted matchcord on horseback being obvious. On occasion,

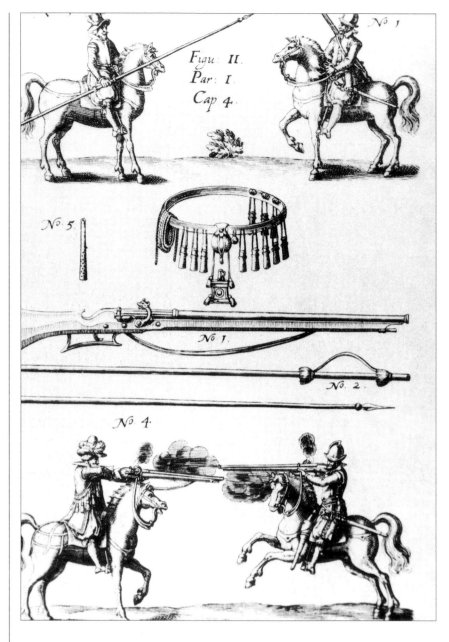

Dragoons. Illustration from Johann Jacobi von Walhausen *Kriegkunst zu Pferde*. Dragoons were mounted musketeers. Walhausen set out a thorough description of the role of the dragoon but added his personal theory on the potential use of mounted pikemen.

cavalry carbines were issued but the preferred weapon was always the musket as this gave the range and killing power required from Dragoons.

Records of the issue of military supplies to Royalist Dragoons show that most, perhaps all, were equipped with matchlock muskets. The Parliamentarian Dragoons were probably equipped with flintlock muskets; certainly they were able to provide flintlock muskets for their artillery guards.

The Train of Artillery

The main responsibility of the Train of Artillery was the cannon used in the field by each army, and the heavier cannon used for siege warfare. Most seventeenth-century cannon were heavy pieces and would be sited during an army's initial deployment but not moved during a battle.

A satirical pamphlet showing clerics as artillerymen. A useful contemporary English illustration of a field artillery piece.

Some commanders made use of lighter artillery, particularly those like the Scots who were strongly influenced by service in the Swedish Army. The Train was also responsible for supplying ammunition for cavalry, infantry and artillery, spare and repaired weapons, artillery tools and the wide variety of equipment an army required in the field.

OPPOSING ARMIES AND FORMATIONS

The battlefield tactics used during the English Civil War do not exist in isolation, they are part of the military practice which developed in western Europe during a series of wars during the sixteenth and seventeenth centuries. The most significant were the Dutch Revolt in the Low Countries (1567-1648), the French Wars of Religion (1562-98) and the Fronde (1648-53), and the Thirty Years War (1618-48). The latter is commonly thought of as a German war but its campaigns ranged over Denmark, Bohemia, northern Italy, the borders of France and the northern frontier of Spain.

Protestant Englishmen, Welshmen and Scots had served as allies and mercenaries in Dutch armies fighting against the Spanish Empire and in several Protestant armies during the Thirty Years War. In particular numerous Scots served as officers in the Swedish Army under Gustavus Adolphus. Smaller numbers of Catholic Englishmen and Irishmen had served in Spanish armies. Englishmen did not develop radically new tactics during the Civil War or the associated wars in Scotland and Ireland, but by 1644 they had become as effective in using the tactics of their time as the best soldiers in Europe.

Harquebusier. This class of cavalryman was originally used for firepower support for cuirassiers. Harquebusiers were cheaper to equip than cuirassiers and by the 1630s commanders were using harquebusiers as part of their main battle cavalry.

Battle Formations

In 1642 an English commander's choice of the battle formation for his army was based on one of the four main models then in use by Protestant armies. This was not simply a choice of one of four formations as variations existed for each and innovative commanders would develop changes of their own. The choice of a style of battle formation represents the commander's preference and was the necessary starting point for the deployments he hoped to use in battle. The European commanders who created these models, such as the Dutch Prince Maurice of Nassau and the Swedish King Gustavus Adolphus, were noted for the care they took to train their men in their chosen battle formations by carrying out military exercises involving the whole army.

Having drawn up the battle plan he had chosen, the commander may have made alterations during the campaign in response to changes in the size of his army, such as a large detachment or the addition of fresh troops, or following intelligence on the size and composition of the opposing army. He would also have had to consider changes, if he had time, once he had seen the ground on which he intended to fight or had received advice from his scouts on the enemy position he was to attack.

The Dutch styles

The origin of all four models of battle formation lies in Prince Maurice's Dutch Army reforms. As with most of their reforms, the Dutch drew inspiration from classical Greek and Roman military systems but adapted them to take account of developments in military theory and practice and weapons.

The two most common deployments used by the Dutch Army are illustrated. Both remained the basis of Dutch theory during the 1630s as the Dutch Army continued to use these formations rather than copy those introduced by the Swedish King Gustavus Adolphus.

The Swedish style

The third Protestant model was Gustavus Adolphus's Swedish infantry brigade formation. The accompanying illustration shows both versions used by the Swedish Army. The first was a brigade of four squadrons used between 1628 and 1631 and the second was a brigade of three squadrons

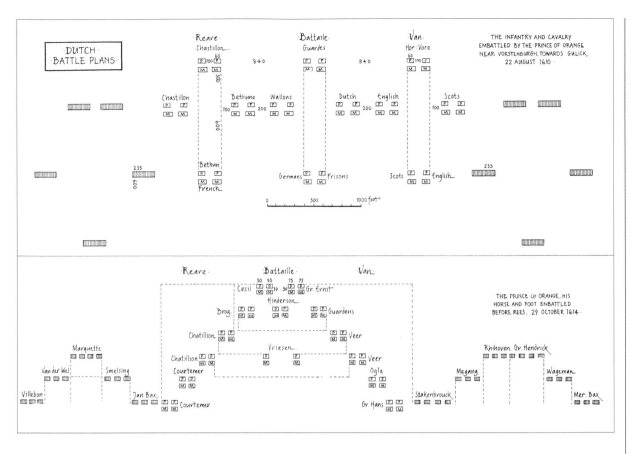

Showing the deployments of the Dutch armies commanded by The Prince of Orange at Vorstenburgh and Rees. These were the two most common deployments used by the Dutch Army. (Derek Stone)

first developed during 1627–28 and used again between 1631 and 1634 when a shortage of pikemen made it necessary to do without the fourth, reserve, squadron.

Gustavus Adolphus was killed at the height of his fame as his army defeated Albrecht von Wallenstein at the battle of Lützen in 1632. Within two years of Gustavus Adolphus's death Swedish forces abandoned the Swedish brigade style. This may have been because in order to be effective it required a high percentage of experienced or veteran officers, sergeants and soldiers.

The German style

The Swedish model had been spectacularly successful in Gustavus Adolphus's great victory over the Imperialist army at the Battle of Breitenfeld in 1631. Imperialist officers excused their defeat on the grounds that their over-confident commander Jean 't Serclaes, Count Tilly, had mounted an all-out attack with no reserve. However, they reviewed the size of their infantry formations and the Imperialist commander Albrecht von Wallenstein's battle plan for the later stages of his campaign in 1632 showed infantry drawn up in smaller units and in three successive lines.

Thereafter both Protestant and Imperialist armies adopted a style, based on the use of a series of infantry units formed in two or three successive lines, which could be described as a German style as it evolved during the Thirty Years War in Germany. The illustration based on Wallenstein's plan shows an example of the fourth model deployment.

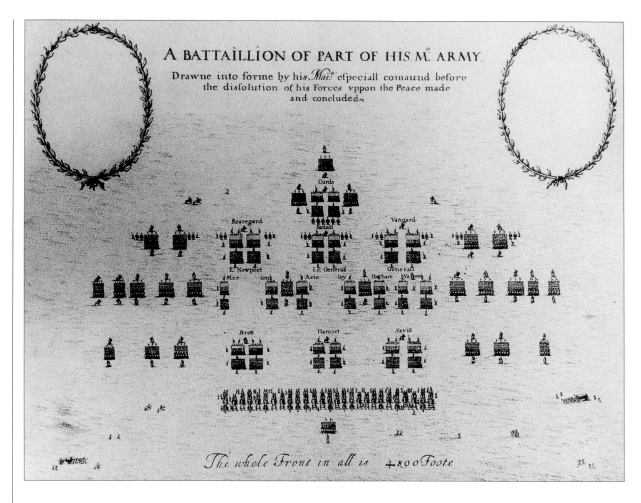

A demonstration of the battle deployment of the King's army during the Bishops Wars. This demonstrates the Dutch influence on English military theory immediately before the Civil War.

There are still variations, for example the Imperialists retain a preference for larger formations, but essentially both Protestant and Catholic armies were using similar formations by the later 1630s.

The Cavalry

Cavalry deployed in the Dutch, Swedish or German styles was formed of squadrons composed of several troops of Horse in two or three successive lines. There was some debate in western Europe over the size of the squadrons, some commanders preferring the strength of a few large squadrons whilst others favoured the greater flexibility of a large number of smaller squadrons. The Dutch practice for cavalry was to deploy them in a chequerboard pattern similar to that of their infantry, usually with a regiment in a line of several separate troops. Both the Swedish and the Imperialists preferred to use larger squadrons each formed of several troops.

By 1642 Swedes and Imperialists used both the Dutch chequerboard deployment and an alternative which placed their second line cavalry squadrons directly behind those in the first line. The rationale behind this change was that whereas infantry formations could retreat by an about turn, cavalry had to wheel and if deployed in a chequerboard pattern they would wheel directly into their second line. The risk of a shattered first line of cavalry breaking up its supporting line was reduced by placing the second line units directly behind those in the first.

OPPOSITE **The three and four squadron brigades as used by the Swedish Army. Within two years of the death of Gustavus Adolphus at Lützen in 1632 the Swedish brigade had been abandoned. (Derek Stone)**

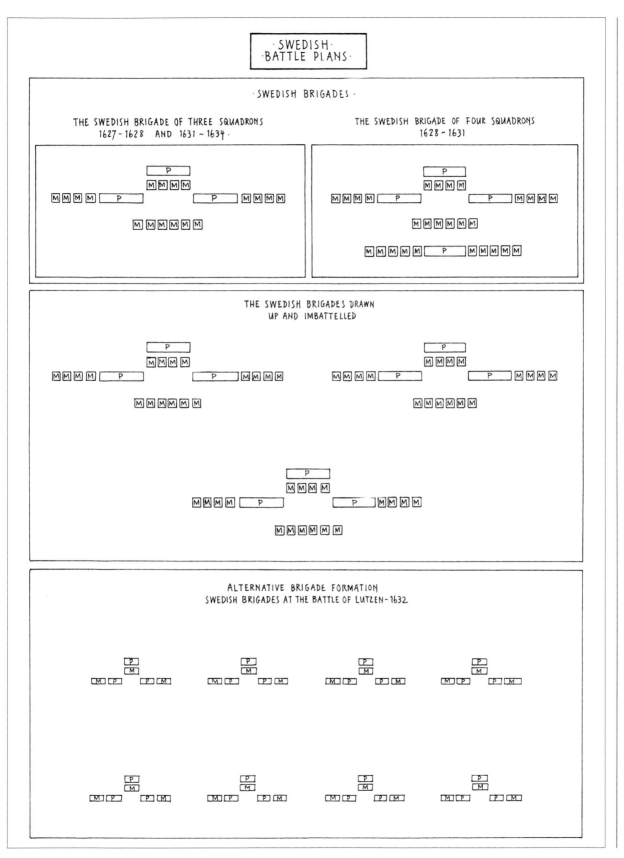

· SWEDISH ·
· BATTLE PLANS ·

· SWEDISH BRIGADES ·

THE SWEDISH BRIGADE OF THREE SQUADRONS
1627 - 1628 AND 1631 ~ 1634 ·

THE SWEDISH BRIGADE OF FOUR SQUADRONS
1628 ~ 1631

THE SWEDISH BRIGADES DRAWN
UP AND IMBATTELLED

ALTERNATIVE BRIGADE FORMATION
SWEDISH BRIGADES AT THE BATTLE OF LUTZEN ~ 1632

Wallenstein's Imperialist battle plan as used in 1632. A modified form of this plan was used at the battle of Lützen. The Imperial or German style had been adapted as a result of the defeats suffered against the Swedes. Imperial armies retained a preference for larger units. This example is based on the original plan found on the body of the Imperialist general, Gottfried Heinrich, Count Pappenheim after the battle of Lützen. (Derek Stone)

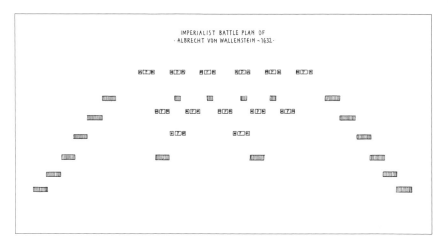

An illustration of musketeer's equipment from John Bingham's *The Tacticks of Aelian*. Most musketeers would have carried these heavy muskets at the outbreak of the Civil War. Few musketeers on either side would have worn helmets during the Civil War.

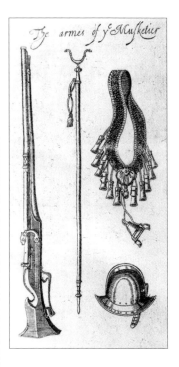

Commanders saw the value that mutual support by infantry and cavalry offered. A commander could deploy troops of cavalry among his infantry lines or units of musketeers seconded from his infantry regiments to serve alongside his cavalry squadrons. The objective of the former was to cover the retreat of his own defeated infantry or exploit success if they were victorious. An incidental effect was that cavalry deployed behind an infantry formation was screened from the main body of opposing cavalry. The English professional soldier Henry Hexham commented on the advantages of this as used in the Dutch Army, writing that 'if an Enemies Horse should be ranged between his Battaillons of foote, it is needfull then, that the other side should observe the same forme likewise, and to have horse to encounter horse, least they should breake in among the foot divisions, & so by this meanes they may with the more convenience second, and relieve one an other, otherwise the Foote being overlayd with an Enemies Horse, having no Horse at hand, to charge and second them, might be easily routed and overthrown'. The Imperialist general Raimondo Monteccucoli writing circa 1642 commented that 'a small squadron of cavalry, acting promptly, can wreak great havoc amongst large infantry battle lines', particularly if the infantry formation was disordered through error or chance, poor leadership or insufficiently trained men. European commanders regarded this as such a useful tactic that they would deploy some of their best cavalrymen for this role.

To support their cavalry wings commanders added infantry firepower support either by placing musketeers or Dragoons on the flanks of the cavalry, using any available cover, or by copying a Swedish tactic that placed groups of musketeers between the cavalry squadrons. Some commanders did both. By 1632 the Swedish had begun to make use of light artillery to support their cavalry in addition to using groups of musketeers.

UNIT STRUCTURE AND STRENGTH

Both cavalry and infantry regiments were organised in brigades as a tactical group with the senior Colonel usually being the brigade commander. Battle orders were given to the brigade commanders, who deployed their men according to the battle plan set out by their

Harquebusier firing a carbine. Detail from John Cruso's *Militarie Instructions for the Cavall'rie*, a book widely used by cavalry officers on both sides.

Printed by the Print[e]

Camb

commander. Henry Hexham commented that the Dutch Army divided its infantry 'into three parts called Brigadoes or Tercias, each of them having a several name, to witt, the Vantguard, the Battell, & the Reereguard'. In the Dutch Army these brigades were formed one alongside the other so that each had regiments in each of the three lines. The objective was, as the English military author John Cruso wrote, to ensure that each unit 'shall be seconded by those of their own squadron, or division, which will give them more courage and assurance'. The Swedish Army also organised their infantry in brigades for battle but deployed them differently. As the illustration shows, a Swedish brigade was not split between the two battle lines, each brigade forming part of one line.

The preferred strength of a battalion in the Dutch service was 'accounted to be 500 pikes & Musketteires, that is, 25 files of Pikes, and 25 files of Musketteires, or more or lesse of the one or the other, as they fall out', the depth of a file in the Dutch service being ten men. In the Dutch Army a battalion was sometimes separated into two or more divisions. These divisions were usually drawn up in pairs one alongside the other because 'two of them being joyned neere one another, can best second, and relieve each other'. The Earl of Essex followed this practice with his own regiment at Edgehill. By the 1630s the Imperial Army had adopted a style of deployment based upon Dutch and Swedish models

29

CAVALRY DEPLOYMENTS.

DUTCH STYLE CAVALRY DEPLOYMENT.

THE FORM OF THE DUKE OF BRUNSWYCKS HORSE BATTAILE
IN THE PLAINE OF ELTON. THE 5ᵗʰ OF SEPTEMBER 1623.

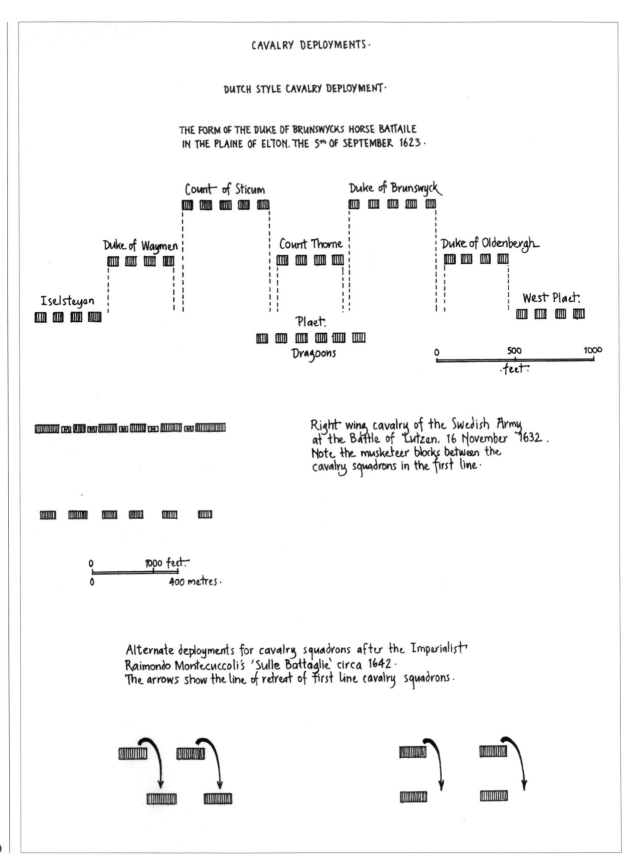

Right wing cavalry of the Swedish Army
at the Battle of Lützen. 16 November 1632.
Note the musketeer blocks between the
cavalry squadrons in the first line.

Alternate deployments for cavalry squadrons after the Imperialist
Raimondo Montecuccoli's 'Sulle Battaglie' circa 1642.
The arrows show the line of retreat of first line cavalry squadrons.

but still preferred large units and German regiments were commonly deployed in a single body. Either style could be used by the English circa 1642. The battalion itself was the battlefield formation and could be formed of a single regiment, part of a single regiment, or a combination of several weak regiments.

By 1642 Imperialist cavalry were deployed in squadrons of between 200 and 300 horsemen formed four or five deep while Swedish squadrons were the same size, 200 or 300 strong but drawn up three deep. The Dutch favoured a number of smaller squadrons, 70 to 80 strong, deployed alongside one another in groups of three or four.

In 1642 Dutch cavalry were deployed five deep, although there was debate amongst those, like the English, who copied the Dutch style but preferred six deep as 'the number of 5 is not divisible by 2, and so in doubling of ranks, or half files, or the like, there is alwaies an odde rank'.

In 1642 an English infantry regiment was composed of several companies and a headquarters. The best regimental structure was considered to be either ten equal companies of 100 men or an unequal pattern of ten companies with the Colonel's company having 200 men, the Lieutenant-Colonel's 160, the Sergeant-Major's 140 and each of the remaining seven companies having 100 men.

Cavalry regiments were formed on a similar model – several troops of horse and a headquarters. The regimental structure was less formal amongst the cavalry than the infantry and it was still common practice to raise independent troops as well as full regiments. In 1642 a regiment usually had six or seven troops. In Essex's army each troop of harquebusiers had a nominal strength of 60 troopers plus 11 officers and each troop of cuirassiers either 100 or 80 troopers plus 12 officers. Commissions for Royalist regiments of Horse refer to 500 Horse as the strength and this may indicate that the intention was for a higher strength of men on the troop, possibly six troops with 80 troopers plus officers in each.

Regiments of Dragoons comprised a headquarters and several companies. In theory a full regiment followed the infantry model and consisted of ten companies but very few ever did. Each company had a model organisation of 100 Dragoons and 11 officers.

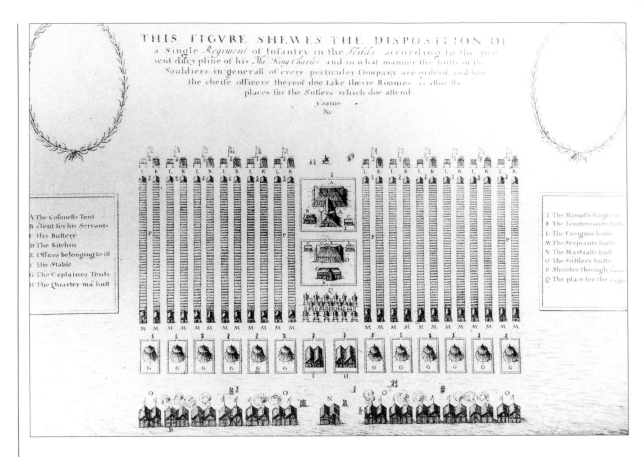

A The Colonells Tent
B A Tent for his Servants
C His Buttery
D The Kitchin
E Offices belonging to it
F His Stable
G The Captaines Tents
H The Quarter ma. hutt

I The Minist̄s Surgeons
K The Levetennants hutts
L The Ensignes hutts
M The Serjeants hutts
N The Martialls hutt
O The Sutlers hutts
P Streetes through the
Q The place for the

Neither infantry nor cavalry models were necessarily the reality as some officers were more successful than others in raising men. An indication that some units were below strength was the Parliament ordinance of 23 September 1642 which ordered that 'such Regiments of Foot as consist of Four hundred Men or more, and Troops of Horse that consist of Forty or more' should march to join the Lord General, the Earl of Essex.

An infantry regiment of the King's army encamped during the Bishops Wars. This is laid out according to the European model for a regiment encamped for the longer term. An army on the march found its billets in the villages and towns on its route.

UNIT FORMATIONS

Contemporary reports of the depth of infantry and cavalry formations on this campaign provide an indication of the deployment each army commander favoured. The Dutch retained a depth of ten men for their infantry formations but developing theories in northern Europe recommended the use of eight or six men. The Swedish used six men in their formations. During the 1630s the English followed Dutch military theory but more progressive commanders had begun to use eight rather than ten as the depth for their infantry formations. As previously detailed, the depth of cavalry formations was usually five deep in the Dutch service although some English officers preferred six deep. Swedish cavalry fought three deep. The Imperialists favoured four or five deep.

The Royalist Sir Richard Bulstrode, who served in the Prince of Wales's regiment of Horse, wrote in his memoirs that 'Our whole Army was drawn up in a body, the Horse Three deep in each Wing, and the

Foot in the Center Six deep.' This is a clear indication that Prince Rupert's orders for Edgehill were based on the Swedish practice.

A comment by Nehemiah Wharton, a sergeant in Colonel Denzil Holles's infantry regiment in the Earl of Essex's army, referring to the poor conditions of their quarters, described the lice which infested the soldiers as 'backbiters' which 'have been seen to march upon some of them six on breast and eight deep at their own open order'. Wharton is using a military analogy to describe the lice at full strength showing that the preferred formation was six files of eight men each for the divisions in Holles's regiment, and probably throughout Essex's army. An eight deep formation showed Essex's infantry using the latest English version of the Dutch model.

There is no comparable evidence for the depth of cavalry formations in Essex's army at Edgehill, although evidence for the battle of Roundway Down (1643) shows Parliament cavalry deployed to fight six deep. It is probable that the Earl of Essex's cavalry used the same six deep formation at Edgehill.

The basic fighting space required for an infantryman, either musketeer or pikeman, was described as 'order'. For an infantryman it was three feet per man, including the ground he stood on. However, the frontage of the infantry formations was more than three feet for every man in the front line as musketeers were formed in blocks with six-foot intervals between them. The basic fighting space required for a cavalryman is also described as 'order', but there was a difference in the way it was measured. The English writer John Cruso described this as 'here we must observe a difference between the manner of taking the distance of the Cavallrie, and that of the Infanterie: for in the foot, the distance is taken from the center of the Souldiers bodie which here cannot be so understood, but onely of the space between horse and horse'. The space a cavalryman requires is the ground occupied by his horse plus three feet.

Commanders in this period used this principle to assess how much space they needed to deploy their men but did not measure exactly in the field. Instead they used a rough and ready method to estimate their frontages. There was some contemporary debate over the measurement but we have followed Sir James Turner's method which allowed four feet for each infantryman in the front line and four feet for each cavalryman. In each case this takes account of the number of soldiers and does not include officers.

DEPLOYMENT AT EDGEHILL

It is necessary to understand the contemporary military systems to appreciate the aims of each commander and how he hoped to deploy his men to best advantage. The military style of the commander was the deciding factor in the deployment of his army. He was constrained by the number of men he had available, their training and experience, but his chosen military style remained the dominant factor.

The Army of Parliament
The main influence on English military theory and practice before the Civil War had been the Dutch model developed by Prince Maurice of

Basil, Lord Feilding. Colonel of a regiment of Parliament cavalry at Edgehill. His father, William, Earl of Denbigh, fought at Edgehill on the other side as a volunteer in the King's Lifeguard of Horse.

The first illustrated training instructions for handling musket and pike printed in England (circa 1617). The illustrations were copied from Johann Jacobi von Walhausen's *Kriegkunst zu Fuss* (Oppenheim, 1616).

Nassau, so much so that the military manuals issued for the militia and used by English armies were copied directly from those in use by the Dutch Army. The actual military experience of the Parliament Commander, the Earl of Essex, had been service in the Dutch Army and the military experience of the majority of his officers, gained professionally or through militia training, was in the Dutch style. However, while the contemporary descriptions of his deployment show that Essex followed the principles of Dutch military theory, he did not use either of the two classic Dutch deployments which we have illustrated.

Although Essex's army would have had a set battlefield plan for deployment during the campaign, he was not in a position to use it at Edgehill as he had to draw up his men to fight while several regiments were still on the march. Contemporary accounts give varying reports on the number of units actually present at the beginning of the battle, some confusion arising because several units arrived during the fighting. It is probable that Essex had 12 regiments of Foot, 42 troops of Horse and 16 pieces of artillery at Edgehill.

Essex and his senior officers had to decide quickly how to deploy their men, and they evidently made a professional job of it. The Royalist Earl of Clarendon commented that 'the earl with great dexterity performed whatsoever could be expected from a wise general'. Orders were drawn up and passed to the infantry brigade commanders and the officers commanding the cavalry on each wing. We have evidence of this from Sir James Ramsey, commander of the cavalry on the left wing, who stated at his court-martial that he had received orders 'for the ordering and commanding of the left Wing of the Cavallery, I did accordingly put them in a position both Defensive and Offensive, interlining the Squadrons with a convenient number of Musqueteers'.

The Royalist Sir Richard Bulstrode's account gives us an impression of the overall deployment and refers to the Parliament commanders having 'all the morning to draw up their Army, in a great plain Field, which they did to their best Advantage, by putting several Bodies of Foot with Retrenchments and Cannon before them, with Intervals betwixt each Body, for their Horse to enter, if need required, and upon their right Wing were some Briars covered with Dragoons'.

Essex's battle plan has not survived but it is possible to reconstruct it by comparing contemporary accounts with the European practice described above and we have illustrated our opinion of how it might have appeared. Bulstrode's account would fit a deployment in the Dutch style or one of the German variants described and illustrated above. Essex appears to have used elements of both the Dutch and German styles for his deployment, placing seven regiments from two of his brigades in his front line and four regiments of his third brigade together with one regiment of another in his second line. As his second line infantry would be placed to cover the spaces, this would require another six units to cover each space. One account refers to a division of Essex's own, large, regiment which suggests that it was formed in two bodies or Grand Divisions. If so, Essex's regiment could either be formed in two bodies side by side, as shown in our illustration of the Dutch model, or deployed as two separate units. We have shown the second alternative in our reconstruction.

The Army of Parliament at the Battle of Edgehill showing the deployment of the 12 regiments of foot, with the Lord General's Regiment split into two Grand Divisions. This battle plan also shows Ramsey's left-wing horse deployed in the Swedish style with commanded musketeers supporting the first line cavalry. Balfour's right-wing horse are shown deployed in the Dutch style. (Derek Stone)

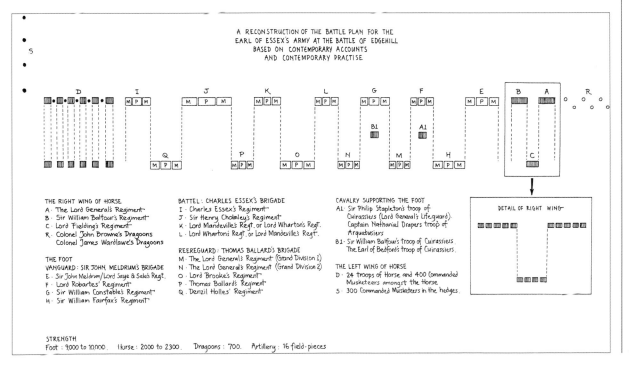

A RECONSTRUCTION OF THE BATTLE PLAN FOR THE EARL OF ESSEX'S ARMY AT THE BATTLE OF EDGEHILL BASED ON CONTEMPORARY ACCOUNTS AND CONTEMPORARY PRACTISE

THE RIGHT WING OF HORSE
A · The Lord General's Regiment
B · Sir William Balfour's Regiment
C · Lord Fielding's Regiment
R · Colonel John Browne's Dragoons
   Colonel James Wardlawe's Dragoons

THE FOOT
VANGUARD: SIR JOHN MELDRUM'S BRIGADE
E · Sir John Meldrum/Lord Saye & Sele's Regt.
F · Lord Robartes' Regiment
G · Sir William Constable's Regiment
H · Sir William Fairfax's Regiment

BATTEL: CHARLES ESSEX'S BRIGADE
I · Charles Essex's Regiment
J · Sir Henry Cholmley's Regiment
K · Lord Mandeville's Regt. or Lord Wharton's Regt.
L · Lord Wharton's Regt. or Lord Mandeville's Regt.

REEREGUARD: THOMAS BALLARD'S BRIGADE
M · The Lord General's Regiment (Grand Division 1)
N · The Lord General's Regiment (Grand Division 2)
O · Lord Brooke's Regiment
P · Thomas Ballard's Regiment
Q · Denzil Holles' Regiment

CAVALRY SUPPORTING THE FOOT
A1· Sir Philip Stapleton's troop of Cuirassiers (Lord General's Lifeguard). Captain Nathaniel Draper's troop of Arquebusiers
B1· Sir William Balfour's troop of Cuirassiers. The Earl of Bedford's troop of Cuirassiers.

THE LEFT WING OF HORSE
D · 24 troops of Horse and 400 Commanded Musketeers amongst the Horse
5 · 300 Commanded Musketeers in the hedges.

DETAIL OF RIGHT WING

STRENGTH
Foot : 9,000 to 10,000. Horse : 2000 to 2300. Dragoons : 700. Artillery : 16 field-pieces

35

CHAP. LXXV.

Of the Horne-battel, how to make it, and to reduce it by firing.

THe *Horne-battel* may be for the fame occafion and ufe, as the *firing by two ranks, ten paces advancing before the Front;* and is by fome held more ferviceable ; becaufe that the *Mufquettiers* do their *execution* more roundly, without any intermiffion of time, and keep themfelves without ftragling from their *Bodies.* Befides, the *Wings of Mufquet-tiers,* being fo advanced, are more apt for *over-fronting,* and more eafily to be wheeled, whereby to charge the Enemy in *flank :* each of thefe *Wings* or *Divifions* are to be led up by a *Serjeant* (or fome other fuperiour *Officer*) unto the *place* appointed by the *Chiefe.* But becaufe it may be performed in time of *exercife,* by the intelligible *Souldier,* obferve the *Command* which produceth this following *Figure.*

Pikes ftand, Mufquettiers martch, until the bringers-up rank with the Front of Pikes.

The *Horn-battel.*

```
    ↳ Ƶ                              Ƶ ↰
S  W M M M M  2          ᴣ  M M M M  W  S
   W M M M M  3   Front  3  M M M M  W
     M M M M  4          4  M M M M
     M M M M  5          5  M M M M
     M M M M  6          6  M M M M
     M M M M  7          7  M M M M
     M M M M  8    E C   8  M M M M
S  • • • • D P P P P P P P P D • • • •  S
           P P P P P P P P
           P P P P P P P P
           P P P P P P P P
           P P P P P P P P
           P P P P P P P P
           P P P P P P P P
         D P P P P P P P P D
                 L.
```

The *Figure* being perfect, the *firft-rank of Mufquettiers prefent, and give fire, wheeling-off* either all to the *right,* or to the *right and left,* (according as they fhall have direction) placing themfelves orderly, in the *Reere* of their own *files.* The *next rank* (after the fame manner) *firing and wheeling-off,* and placing themfelves behind thofe which were their *leaders.* Thus is every *rank,* fucceffively, to do the like, until they have all *given fire.* If the *Commander* would ftill preferve and continue the fame *Figure,* then let the *Mufquettiers* ftill *move forwards,* into the ground (or place) of them that *fired before* them ; and the *forme* will be the fame. But if by the *Chiefetain* it be found neceffary, that after once or twice *firing over,* the *Shot* fhould *flank* their *Pikes,* then the *Mufquet-tiers* muft not advance into their *leaders ground,* but to the contrary, every *rank* is to *pre-fent and fire on the fame ground* they ftand, and that fo foon as they are *clear* of their *lea-ders.* Or, if need be, the *Pikes* may advance and *martch up,* to make their *Front intire :* which being done, the *File-leaders of Mufquettiers* being in *Front,* they are reduced.

The firing defcribed.

Note.

The reduce-ment:

M 3   CHAP.

Infantry firing rank by rank from William Barriffe's *Military Discipline: or, the Young Artillery Man*. Barriffe was Sergeant-Major of John Hamden's infantry regiment which arrived at Edgehill during the closing stages of the Battle.

We have some details of the cavalry deployment on the left wing from the deposition of its commander Sir James Ramsey and his officers at his court-martial. From this we know that he commanded 24 troops of Horse and 700 musketeers drawn from Thomas Ballard's brigade. Ramsey anchored his line on a hedge which flanked his position on the left and placed 300 musketeers there to provide flanking fire to support his main cavalry body. He deployed the remaining 400 'betwixt the Squadrons of Horse'. This deployment follows a style introduced by Gustavus Adolphus and which by 1642 any western European commander might have chosen to use. The cavalry would probably have been deployed in two lines with blocks of musketeers between the squadrons. We do not know whether the cavalry would have been drawn up as individual troops or by combining two or more troops into squadrons. The musketeers would have been deployed in five or six blocks. Placing these in the intervals of the front line would require six or seven squadrons of Horse in the front line. With 24 troops overall, probably deployed in two lines, the most likely option for this wing would be to deploy two troops in each squadron. Ramsey's use of his musketeers suggests that he favoured the Swedish and German styles over the Dutch, so the cavalry may have been drawn up with the squadrons of the second line behind those of the first rather than the Dutch chequerboard pattern.

This leaves 18 troops to be deployed and the account of King James II, who was present at the battle as a boy, states that 'As for their right wing of horse, which were not all come up, they drew up that part off them that was present behind their foot.' The most likely interpretation is that Essex placed three or four troops immediately behind his infantry using one of the popular tactics of the day and the remaining 14 on the right wing. The main deployment of 14 troops would have been set out by Sir William Balfour as individual troops in two lines reflecting his experience in the Dutch service.

Parliamentarian Artillery

Philibert Emmannuel du Bois, Lieutenant-General of the Ordnance was able to establish an artillery train of 29 guns despite the fact that Royalist sympathisers remained in control of the Office of Ordnance until August 1642. His artillery of 29 guns included six mortars and 21 modern field pieces listed as two long- and four short-barrelled 12-pdr cannon, four 6-pdr cannon and eleven 3-pdr 'short drakes'. He was probably able to deploy 16 cannon at Edgehill as six of his 29 pieces were mortars and a further seven were not with Essex's main force.

The King's Army

The Royalist Army shared the same military heritage as the Parliament Army. Its first commander, the Earl of Lindsey, had served in the Dutch Army and the Earl of Clarendon recorded in his *History of the Rebellion* that Lindsey 'preferred the order he had learned under prince Morrice and prince Harry, with whom he had served at the same time when the earl of Essex and he had both had regiments'. In October Clarendon recorded that the Royalist Foot 'were divided into three brigades; the first commanded by sir Nicholas Byron, the second by colonel Harry Wentworth, and the third by Colonel Richard Feilding'. This three-brigade structure follows the classic Dutch model and is evidence that the King's army was initially trained in the Dutch style. The training model followed by the Royalist Army under the Earl of Lindsey would have been similar to that found in the Parliament Army under the Earl of Essex and, left undisturbed, would have turned out a Royalist Army trained to fight in exactly the same way as its Parliament opponents.

Prince Rupert's influence changed this situation as Clarendon recorded that 'the king was so indulgent to him that he took his advice in all things relating to the army, and so upon consideration of their march, and the figure of the battle they resolved to fight in with the enemy, he concurred entirely with prince Rupert's advice, and rejected the opinion of the General' (the Earl of Lindsey). Like many contemporary officers Prince Rupert was strongly influenced by the great victories of Gustavus Adolphus and saw an opportunity to win the war in one stroke by winning a decisive battle. Prince Rupert based his 'figure of battle' or battle formation upon the Swedish model. The

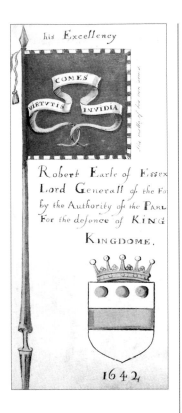

The Earl of Essex's Cornet. The motto 'virtutis comes invidia' translates as 'envy is a companion of virtue'. (Dr Williams Library)

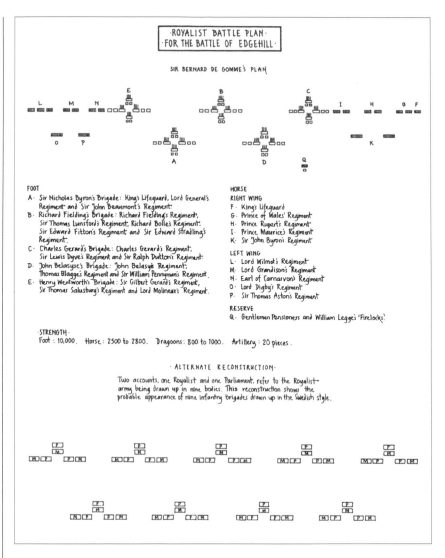

The Royalist Battle Plan for the Battle of Edgehill. The top plan is taken from Sir Bernard de Gomme's contemporary plan. This shows the Royalist infantry deployed in the early four-unit diamond pattern devised for the Swedish brigades before they landed in Germany. The lower plan is a reconstruction based on two contemporary accounts referring to nine bodies of Royalist Foot. This plan shows a deployment based on the Swedish three-unit brigade. (Derek Stone)

underlying structure of infantry units and troops of Horse are similar but the deployment and tactical style are quite different and Prince Rupert was dependent on assistance from Patrick Ruthven and other officers with experience in the Swedish Army.

A copy of the Royalist headquarters plan made by Sir Bernard de Gomme, one of Prince Rupert's officers, survives entitled as the plan of the Royalist Army at the battle of Edgehill. Two Royalist memoirs also record that Prince Rupert deployed his infantry according to the Swedish brigade model. The first of these, by the future King James II, recorded 'the foot was drawn up that day much differing from the manner now in use, but according to the Swedish Brigade as they then called it'. However, de Gomme remained associated with Royalists in exile, including James himself, and it is probable that James's recollection of the battle formation was based on de Gomme's plan or a copy of it. The second account is by John Belasyse and this provides independent evidence as he recalled that the order of battle 'had been formerly designed by General Ruthin (Ruthven), Sir Arthur Aston and Sir Jacob Ashley (Astley), which was in several brigades, after the Swedish way'.

A satirical pamphlet dated 1641. The intention was to show the licentious nature of professional or mercenary soldiers. The illustration is based on a popular subject for Dutch paintings at the time, a soldier engaged in seduction or being entertained by a harlot. (British Library)

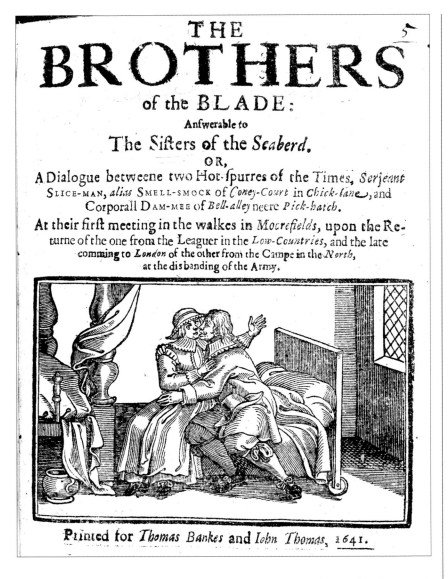

THE BROTHERS
of the BLADE:
Anfwerable to
The Sifters of the Scaberd.
OR,
A Dialogue betweene two Hot-fpurres of the Times, Serjeant SLICE-MAN, alias SMELL-SMOCK of Coney-Court in Chick-lane, and Corporall DAM-MEE of Bell-alley neere Pick-hatch.
At their firft meeting in the walkes in Mocrefields, upon the Re-turne of the one from the Leaguer in the Low-Countries, and the late comming to London of the other from the Campe in the North, at the disbanding of the Army.

Printed for Thomas Bankes and Iohn Thomas, 1641.

De Gomme's plan shows that the version used was the four unit diamond pattern devised for Gustavus' infantry before it landed in Germany and not the three unit arrow-head style commonly used later by the Swedish armies. There is conflicting evidence over the precise deployment used on the day. Although de Gomme's plan shows five brigades both John Belasyse, who was one of the Royalist brigade commanders, and the official account sent to the Parliament by six Parliament officers immediately after the battle comment that the Royalist infantry was drawn up in nine bodies, Belasyse commenting that the foot were 'divided into nine bodies vitz: five in front and four in reserve' while the Parliament officers reported that they observed the Royalist infantry 'divided into nine great Bodies'. However, there is also evidence to support the accuracy of de Gomme's plan as a copy of Prince Rupert's deployment on the day of the battle of Edgehill, as de Gomme showed the King's Lifeguard of Horse placed on the furthest right of the Royalist right wing. The Lifeguard troopers had requested permission to fight in the front line at Edgehill and prove themselves to be fighting

Cavalry combat. Prince Rupert's instructions to his troopers at Edgehill were to save their pistols until they 'broke in amongst the Enemy'.

men because of 'a little provocation, or for a word of distaste the day before, or being called, The Troop of Shew' or 'out of their desire for glory'. Clarendon recorded that this change to the planned deployment was made 'at the entrance into the field', meaning the battlefield.

The Swedish influence on Prince Rupert's cavalry tactics can be seen in his battlefield instructions to his cavalrymen 'to march as close as was possible, keeping their Ranks with Sword in Hand, to receive the Enemy's Shot without firing either Carbin or Pistol, till we broke in amongst the Enemy, and then make use of our Fire-Arms as need should require'. This advice resembled the Swedish practice at the battle of Breitenfeld (1631) described by Robert Munro in his account of service in the Swedish Army: 'the resolution of our horsemen on this service was praiseworthy, seeing they never loosed a pistol at the enemy till first they had discharged theirs'.

Royalist artillery

Sir John Heydon, Lieutenant of the Ordnance and effective commander of the artillery had more difficulty in establishing an artillery train than his Parliamentary counterpart. Heydon had 20 artillery pieces at Edgehill, 14 of them field pieces. Some of these would have been the 'seven or eight field-pieces' sent from Holland by Queen Henrietta Maria, others may have been of older patterns. Surviving records maintained by Edward Sherburne, one of Heydon's officers, give the Royalist field artillery available for Edgehill as six 'fawcons', six 'fawconnets', two 'rabonetts' together with six heavier pieces – two 'demi-cannon', two 'culverin' and two 'demi-culverin'.

THE CAMPAIGN

Sir John Hotham, Governor of Kingston upon Hull. Hotham's refusal to allow the King and his followers to enter Hull denied them arms that they desperately needed to equip the newly raised Royalist Army.

The King was able to raise the Yorkshire Trained Bands, but they refused to serve outside their own county. On 29 April 1642 the fledgling Royal Army appeared before Hull, which contained military supplies that would have overcome the shortages which limited the fighting power of the Royalist Foot at Edgehill. Unfortunately for the King, the governor of Hull, Sir John Hotham, had thrown in his lot with Parliament and the city gates remained firmly barred. Charles was forced into a humiliating withdrawal.

In June, frustrated both in his attempts to muster the Trained Bands in counties other than Yorkshire and to persuade the Yorkshire Trained Bands to serve outside the county, the King began to issue Commissions of Array to county authorities and to grant commissions as officers to individuals.

The King advanced from York to Nottingham, within striking range of the Parliamentarian towns of Birmingham, Coventry and Northampton. On 22 August the Royal Standard was raised on castle hill at Nottingham with much pomp and ceremony. A storm blew it to the ground that night, an omen remembered by many once the war was lost.

The King's standard was formally raised in Nottingham on 25 August 1642. It was 'blown down the same night it had been set up'. A poor omen for the start of a civil war.

Nottingham

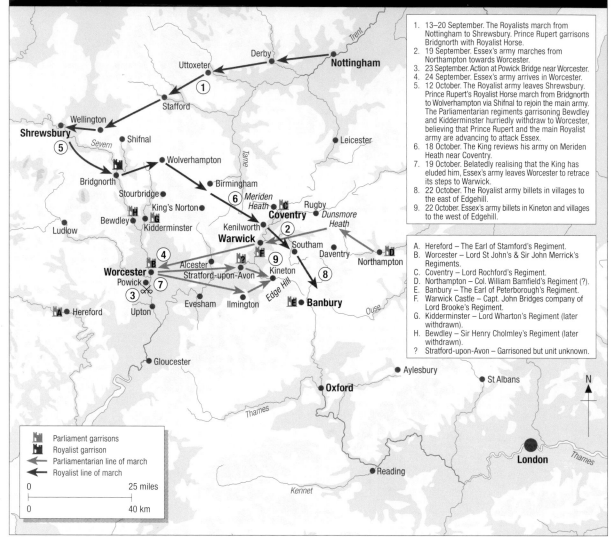

1. 13–20 September. The Royalists march from Nottingham to Shrewsbury. Prince Rupert garrisons Bridgnorth with Royalist Horse.
2. 19 September. Essex's army marches from Northampton towards Worcester.
3. 23 September. Action at Powick Bridge near Worcester.
4. 24 September. Essex's army arrives in Worcester.
5. 12 October. The Royalist army leaves Shrewsbury. Prince Rupert's Royalist Horse march from Bridgnorth to Wolverhampton via Shifnal to rejoin the main army. The Parliamentarian regiments garrisoning Bewdley and Kidderminster hurriedly withdraw to Worcester, believing that Prince Rupert and the main Royalist army are advancing to attack Essex.
6. 18 October. The King reviews his army on Meriden Heath near Coventry.
7. 19 October. Belatedly realising that the King has eluded him, Essex's army leaves Worcester to retrace its steps to Warwick.
8. 22 October. The Royalist army billets in villages to the east of Edgehill.
9. 22 October. Essex's army billets in Kineton and villages to the west of Edgehill.

A. Hereford – The Earl of Stamford's Regiment.
B. Worcester – Lord St John's & Sir John Merrick's Regiments.
C. Coventry – Lord Rochford's Regiment.
D. Northampton – Col. William Bamfield's Regiment (?).
E. Banbury – The Earl of Peterborough's Regiment.
F. Warwick Castle – Capt. John Bridges company of Lord Brooke's Regiment.
G. Kidderminster – Lord Wharton's Regiment (later withdrawn).
H. Bewdley – Sir Henry Cholmley's Regiment (later withdrawn).
? Stratford-upon-Avon – Garrisoned but unit unknown.

The Parliamentarian regiment of Denzil Holles MP was ordered to Coventry, which was soon to close its gates on the approach of the King's soldiers. Marching with Holles's regiment was Sergeant Nehemiah Wharton, who as part of a force mustering 3,000 Foot and 400 Horse witnessed an encounter with the enemy at Southam: 'In the morninge early our enemise, consistinge of about eight hundred horse and three hundred foote, with ordinance … intended to set upon us before wee could gather our companies together, but being ready all night, early in the morning wee went to meet them with a few troops of horse and six feild peeces, and beigne on fier to be at them wee marched thorow the corne and got the hill of them, whereupon they played upon us with their ordinances, but they came short. Our gunner tooke their owne bullet, sent it to them againe, and killed a horse and a man. After we gave them eight shot more, whereupon all their foote companies fled and offered their armes in the townes adjacent for twelve pence a peece.' [C.S.P 1641–1643 Vol CCCCXCI]

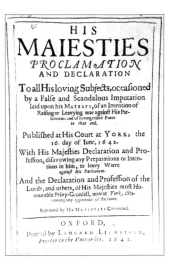

Royalist pamphlet printed by the King's Printer in Oxford. The King's declaration at York on 16 June 1642 that he had no intention to go to war against the Parliament.

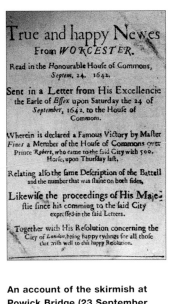

An account of the skirmish at Powick Bridge (23 September 1642) printed in London on 26 September 1642. This places a Parliament 'spin' on the event describing a Royalist victory as if the Parliament had won.

On 9 September amongst a great display of public support the Earl of Essex left London to take command of the gathering Army of Parliament. The following day he established his headquarters at Northampton and it appeared that a clash between the two armies was imminent.

The King had managed to raise only some five regiments of Foot and 500 Horse and desperately needed to increase his strength before he was confronted by Essex. On 13 September the small Royal army left Nottingham and marched via Derby, Uttoxeter, Stafford and Wellington, reaching Shrewsbury on 20 September. Here the King could draw on recruits from North Wales and Lancashire and his numbers grew beyond his capacity to arm them. Prince Rupert with a strong body of Horse was established at Bridgnorth to guard against Essex's advance.

Essex was seeking to prevent both a Royalist advance on London and a recruiting sweep by the King's army down the Welsh borders, via Ludlow, Hereford and Gloucester. Worcester was the obvious position to block such a progress while still offering the opportunity to march quickly back to Warwick should the King head for London. Unfortunately Essex's plans made no allowance for the inability of his outlying garrisons to keep a watch on the King's army, the state of the roads or the lamentably slow progress that his army made on the march.

On 19 September Essex left Northampton for Worcester and the following day met his army gathered for its first muster on Dunsmore Heath near Rugby. Wharton records the scene: 'Tuesday morning our regiment marched two miles unto Dunsmore Heath, where the Lord General and his regiment met us, as also the Lord of Stanford, Colonel Cholmley, and Colonel Hamden, with many troops of horse and eighteen field pieces, where we kept our rendezvous until even, when we had tidings that all the malignants in Worcestershire, with the Cavaliers, were got into Worcester and fortifies themselves.' Through drenching rain and over roads turning to quagmires, Wharton and his comrades followed the army towards Worcester.

POWICK BRIDGE

The Royalist Sir John Byron, with a party of Horse and Dragoons, had been slowly convoying a baggage train carrying contributions from Oxford to be handed to the King at Shrewsbury. On 20 September he reached Worcester and began to fortify the town hoping to peacefully await a relieving force commanded by Prince Rupert which would bring him safely to the King.

By 22 September Rupert had reached Bewdley, but at dawn on that day 1,000 Horse and Dragoons of Essex's army under Colonel John Brown attempted to force entry through the Sidbury gate at Worcester. The Parliamentarians failed to bluff their way in and the alarm was raised against them.

Brown crossed the river Severn by the bridge at Upton and by some nearer fords and moved up the west bank to Powick on the river Teme arriving by dawn on 23 September. He expected that when Essex arrived in strength from the east, Byron would try to escape to the west bank of the Severn putting the river between himself and Essex. By crossing the

A satirical London pamphlet depicting the conflict between Royalists and Cavaliers as a dog fight. The 'pudel' represents Prince Rupert's pet poodle 'Boy'.

river Teme by the bridge at Powick Brown planned to trap Byron. At four in the afternoon Parliamentarian sympathisers alerted Brown to the fact that Byron was preparing to march. Brown ordered Colonel Edwin Sandys to lead the cavalry across Powick Bridge and along a narrow hedged lane to form up in Wick Field while Brown mounted his Dragoons before following him.

Unknown to the Parliamentarians Prince Rupert had arrived in Worcester earlier in the day and his dismounted troops of Horse were resting in Wick Field. Fortunately for the Royalists, Brown's outflanking march was well known in the city and Rupert had lined the hedges leading from Powick Bridge with Dragoons.

Forced into a long column by the narrow bridge and confined lane, Colonel Sandys' Parliamentary troopers were poorly formed to meet the volleys of shot they received in their flanks from the Royalist Dragoons hidden in the hedges. Eager to escape the trap, and unable to turn to retreat, Sandys spurred his men on and they emerged into Wick Field in some confusion. Far from finding an escape from danger they now found Rupert's men hurriedly mounting their horses and forming into troops. The Royalists recovered their composure first and Rupert led them into the charge.

The Parliamentary and Royalist Horse had been trained in the two opposing styles of cavalry combat. Rupert favoured the Swedish-style charge to contact, sword in hand, with the use of pistols reserved for the pursuit. The Parliamentarian cavalry relied on receiving the enemy's charge at the halt, with a well-disciplined volley of carbine and pistol shot to disorder their opponents and break up the impetus of the charge, before falling on with the sword. The latter tactic could work when properly executed as is related by Nathaniel Fiennes in the pamphlet *A Letter Purporting the True Relation of the Skirmish at Worcester* which described his experiences at Powick Bridge: 'We let them come up very near that their horses' noses almost touched those of our front rank before ours gave fire, and then [the Parliamentarians] gave fire, and very well to my thinking, with their carbines, after [we] fell in with good hope to have broken them (being pretty well shattered with the first charge of carbines). But of a sudden we found all the troops on both sides of us melted away, and our rear being carried with them.'

44

The Parliamentarians were bundled back down the lane and over Powick Bridge, where Colonel Brown and his Dragoons managed to blunt the Royalist pursuit. This did not stop the Parliamentarian cavalry riding in alarm back across the Severn at Upton and on to Pershore, where their tales of disaster so alarmed the Earl of Essex's own Lifeguard of Horse that they joined in the rout.

THE KING OPENS HIS CAMPAIGN

It took a further two weeks for his army to concentrate and Essex seemed happy to allow the King to make the next move. Expecting the Royal Army to advance towards him down the Severn valley Essex established garrisons at Bewdley and Kidderminster. On 10 October Rupert, with the Royalist Horse, moved to Shifnal and Wolverhampton. By 14 October Rupert had reached Stourbridge and Lord Wharton fell back from Kidderminster giving Essex the erroneous impression that the King was marching towards him at Worcester.

On 12 October 1642 the Royal Army began to march out of Shrewsbury with London as its ultimate objective. Some among the King's Council had proposed a march towards Worcester aiming to bring the Earl of Essex to battle before he could concentrate his forces and gather up the reinforcements that Parliament was hurriedly raising in the Home Counties around London.

Such a strategy had its attractions. Essex had marched his army far from its campaign base at Warwick and the depredation of his soldiers had done much to increase the hostility of the local populace who tended to favour the King's cause. The poor condition of the roads between Worcester and Warwick, which were bad even by the standards of the time, had been made critical by the ceaseless rain. An early battle at Worcester would catch Essex isolated from many of the garrisons and

A column of infantry on the march and a troop of cuirassiers. Note the trumpeter.

Sir Thomas Lunsford, Colonel of a Royalist infantry regiment. An archetypal rakehell cavalier once described as a man 'who neither fears God nor man' who had 'given himself over to all lewdness and dissoluteness'.

detachments he had made from his army and if defeated the Parliamentarians would have no base on which to rally.

The tempting picture of the war won at a single stroke was moderated by the image of the King's cause lost in a day. The countryside around Worcester was enclosed with many small fields separated by dense hedges. The King's cavalry, his great strength which it might be hoped would be the decisive force in any major encounter, would be hemmed in and unable to manoeuvre. The countryside through the counties on the road towards London offered open ground where Prince Rupert could destroy the Parliamentarian Horse and cripple their army. Many Royalists anticipated an easy victory wherever the battle was fought and the swift crushing of the revolt by marching on the vipers' nest in London had many attractions.

Essex missed a chance to react when on 17 October Lord Willoughby of Parham marching south of Birmingham fought a sharp encounter with Rupert at Kings Norton.

The 18th of October saw the Royalist Army drawn up on Meriden Heath outside Coventry. The King had stayed at Packington in the house of Sir Robert Fisher where he rejected a petition from both Commons and Lords inviting him to come peacefully to Parliament. He showed his disdain by refusing safe conduct to the Parliamentarian messengers.

Finally on 19 October Essex reacted to the King's marches, which by this time had carried him to Kenilworth, where he was well placed to strike at the many Parliamentarian towns in the area. Essex's army began the march back to its base at Warwick. Progress was agonisingly slow as it was hampered by poor roads, foul weather and an extensive train of baggage and artillery. The faster moving Foot and the Horse spread out the frontage on which they advanced to find easier billets and better chance of plunder. Entering Warwickshire troops spread from Alcester, Great Alne and Studley in the north to Illmington in the south. Arriving in the area to the north-west of the high ridge of Edgehill the Parliamentarian army quartered amongst the local villages and towns of Halford, Pillerton Priors, the Tysoes, Radway and Kineton.

Nine days after leaving Shrewsbury the Royalist Army was making its way from Southam to a rendezvous near the Wormleighton Hills only a few miles north-east of Edgehill. Warwick, with its well-garrisoned castle, had been bypassed but the weaker defences of the Parliamentarian outpost at Banbury offered a chance to open the road to Oxford and undermine Essex's main base at Warwick.

The intention to fall on Banbury had been formed some days previously. Essex had been unaware of the plan or he would have taken the Oxford road from Worcester to make a quicker march to Banbury which would perhaps have allowed him to appear on the ridge at Edgehill to confound the approaching Royalists. As it was the Parliamentary garrison at Warwick discovered documents revealing the King's intentions when part of the Royal baggage train, straying too close to Warwick castle, fell into the hands of a patrol led by Captain John Bridges. A letter giving news of the impending attack on Banbury was read in the House of Commons on 22 October and Essex must also have been informed. On their march back from Worcester several of Essex's senior officers stayed in Stratford-upon-Avon. Essex was not with them and he may have ridden on to Warwick to see the King's despatches for himself.

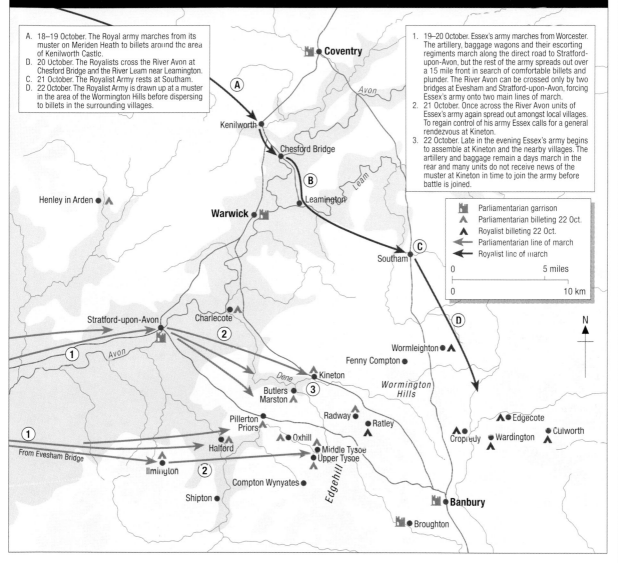

A. 18–19 October. The Royal army marches from its muster on Meriden Heath to billets around the area of Kenilworth Castle.
D. 20 October. The Royalists cross the River Avon at Chesford Bridge and the River Leam near Leamington.
C. 21 October. The Royalist Army rests at Southam.
D. 22 October. The Royalist Army is drawn up at a muster in the area of the Wormington Hills before dispersing to billets in the surrounding villages.

1. 19–20 October. Essex's army marches from Worcester. The artillery, baggage wagons and their escorting regiments march along the direct road to Stratford-upon-Avon, but the rest of the army spreads out over a 15 mile front in search of comfortable billets and plunder. The River Avon can be crossed only by two bridges at Evesham and Stratford-upon-Avon, forcing Essex's army onto two main lines of march.
2. 21 October. Once across the River Avon units of Essex's army again spread out amongst local villages. To regain control of his army Essex calls for a general rendezvous at Kineton.
3. 22 October. Late in the evening Essex's army begins to assemble at Kineton and the nearby villages. The artillery and baggage remain a days march in the rear and many units do not receive news of the muster at Kineton in time to join the army before battle is joined.

Parliamentarian garrison
Parliamentarian billeting 22 Oct.
Royalist billeting 22 Oct.
Parliamentarian line of march
Royalist line of march

| 0 | | 5 miles |
| 0 | | 10 km |

Essex now intended to save Banbury from the Royalists and changed his line of march with Kineton as the next rendezvous for the army. It was the natural assembly point for the army before it undertook the laborious task of hauling its baggage and artillery train up the steep slopes of Edgehill, which lay across the direct line of march from Kineton to Banbury.

THE ARMIES ASSEMBLE FOR BATTLE

On 22 October Lord Digby scouting to the west of the Royalist Army with a party of 400 Royalist Horse failed to detect the Parliament troops in the area of Kineton and reported that there was no sign of the enemy. A Council of War at Edgecote decided that on the next day Sir Nicholas Byron's Brigade of 4,000 men with a train of artillery would attempt to

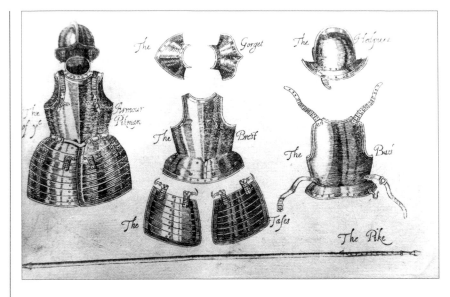

seize Banbury. By nightfall the Royal Army was dispersing amongst the villages around the Wormington Hills. Stretching from Cropredy to Edgecote the King's soldiers dispersed to the most comfortable billet they could find. The King stayed at the home of Sir William Chancie at Edgecote while the Earl of Lindsey was at Culworth and Prince Rupert rode to Wormleighton. His staff, riding ahead of him, surprised and captured a quartermaster's party from Essex's army. Following information gained from these prisoners, Rupert sent a patrol of 24 troopers from his regiment to Kineton. At about midnight the patrol returned with news that the Parliamentarian army was at hand. By three in the morning of 23 October the King was aware that Essex was marching to the relief of Banbury and an hour later tired staff officers were dispatching orders for a general rendezvous on Edgehill.

News of the presence of the Parliamentarian Army so nearby was arriving at the King's headquarters from other sources. Richard Bulstrode records how he spent the night: 'The Prince of Wales's Regiment in which we were, was quartered in two or three Villages under Wormington Hills. When it was dark, we saw several Fires not far from us, and sending out a Party to see, we were soon informed, that the Earl of Essex was there with his whole Army, and quartered at Keinton, a Market-Town. Whereupon our whole Regiment drew into the Fields … and soon after we received Orders to be upon our Guard all Night, and to be the next Morning by Eight, at the Rendezvous upon Wormington Hills.' [Memoirs Part III published 1721]

The march of Essex's army had been even slower than that of the King and his vanguard arrived in Kineton only at nine or ten o'clock on the night of 22 October, with some regiments and a part of the Train of Artillery still many miles behind. At eight on the morning of 23 October 1642, Essex was on his way to church when, 'unexpectedly an Alarme came … that the Enemy was advancing within two or three miles'. The Parliamentarian Officers' account says: 'we intended to rest the Sabbath-day, and the rather, that our Artillery and the forces left with it might come up to us'. [*The Account of the Battel at Edgehill Oct. 23 1642 as publisht by Order of Parliament* – Rushworth III, II, pp 35-39]

Parliament Uniforms

Most Parliament infantry had been issued with coats, shirts, shoes and snapsacks by October 1642, some with caps as well. Each regiment appears to have been issued with coats of the same colour creating a regimental appearance.

Regiments	Coat colour
Sir John Meldrum's Brigade	
Lord Saye and Sele's Regiment	Blue
Lord Robartes' Regiment	Red lined yellow
Sir William Constable's Regiment	Blue
Sir William Fairfax's Regiment	Probably grey
Charles Essex's Brigade	
Charles Essex's Regiment	Tawny lined yellow
Sir Henry Cholmley's Regiment	Blue
Lord Mandeville's Regiment	Blue
Lord Wharton's Regiment	Probably grey
Thomas Ballard's Brigade	
The Lord General's Regiment	Orange
Lord Brooke's Regiment	Purple
Thomas Ballard's Regiment	Grey lined white
Denzil Holles's Regiment	Red

There is no evidence that Royalist infantry had been issued with uniform coats by October 1642

The Royalist John Williams, Archbishop of York, in the guise of the Church Militant. This was carefully focussed Puritan propaganda against the Anglican Williams as this type of image was commonly used to depict Catholic priests oppressing Protestants.

However, Essex may have possessed intelligence of the King's army which he chose not to share even with his senior officers. To jump ahead to events two days after the battle as reported in Prince Rupert's Diary: 'that night the prince with a party of horse followed Essex, and took all his plate, with his Cabinett of Letters, which showed that one Blake (who was with the king) betrayed all his Majesties Counsells, and he was afterwards hanged'. [Part III, Wiltshire Record Office]

If Blake the spy was able to inform Essex that the whole Royalist army was nearby he was not the only source of information. Lord Wharton later reported to Parliament on 22 October that 'all that night newes came that the King was going to Banbury'.

The discovery of Essex's army so close at hand caused consternation amongst the Royalists. Bulstrode records the King's Council of War which now took place: 'It was debated, whether to march towards London, or to march back, and fight the Enemy, who we saw from the Hill, embattelling their Army in the Bottom near Keinton. To march from them was thought dishonourable, as if we feared them, and they would be sure to follow, and give us continual Trouble in our March, when we should not, perhaps find so good Occasion to fight them; and so it was resolved, that we should go down the Hill and attack them.'

Although the Royalists had taken the Parliamentarians unprepared, the delays in gathering their own forces deprived them of the advantage of surprise. The Royalist official account describes the delays in forming up the army: 'The King's Horse came between 10 and 11 a Clock in the Morning, and the Van of Foot came within an hour after, but the Rear (which happened at that time to be the Lord-Lieutenant-General's Regiment) with the Artillery, came not within 2 hours after. As soon as we came to the Top of Edgehill which looks upon Keynton, we saw the Rebels Army drawing out, and setting themselves in Battalia; whereupon

49

A Dutch painting of soldiers relaxing in camp. The bough and the tankard above the tent are the sign of a sutler providing drink, food and entertainment. (National Gallery)

the King's Horse went down the Hill, and set themselves in order; the Foot likewise having Command to come down the Hill, and do the like; but before that was done, and the King's Artillery came, it was past 2 in the Afternoon.' [*A Relation of the Battel fought between Keyton and Edgehill by His Majesty's Army and that of the Rebels; Printed by his Majesty's Command at Oxford by Leonard Lichfield 1642*]

All was not well amongst the King's officers, who had begun to form factions for and against Prince Rupert. Bulstrode relates how these problems came to a head as the army deployed for battle: 'The King desired the Earl of Lindsey, who was his Lieutenant General, that he would permit General Ruthven, an old Scotch Officer, and who had long served under Gustavus Adolphus, the late King of Sweden, and had been a Lieutenant General in his Army, to draw up his Majesty's Army that Day, and to command it, being an old experienced General; to which the Earl of Lindsey (being wholly made of Obedience) willingly complied, and said he would serve the King that Day, as Collonel of the King's Royal Regiment of Foot Guards.'

Lindsey had served many years previously in the Dutch Army and clashed with Prince Rupert, who wished to employ the Swedish tactics he had studied. Lindsey may have been correct as the old Dutch formations were easier for novice officers and newly recruited soldiers to understand. The argument soon degenerated and factions had appeared soon after the army left Shrewsbury as Clarendon relates:

'When the whole army marched together, there was quickly discovered an unhappy jealousy and division between the principal officers, which grew quickly into perfect faction between the foot and the horse. The earl of Lindsey was general of the whole army by his commission, and thought very equal to it. But when prince Rupert came to the King, which was after the standard was set up, and received a commission to be general of horse, which all men knew was designed for him, there was a clause inserted into it which exempted him from receiving orders from any body but from the King himself.' [*The History of the Rebellion and Civil War in England*]

Under the circumstances of this ongoing feud and the constant insult of having his authority as commander ignored, Lindsey's action in standing down from his post can be better understood.

The Battlefield

The long ridge of Edgehill, 700 feet above sea level, played no direct part in the battle. The Royalists formed their battle line on the level ground in front of Radway, occupying a great plain field or 'fair meadow'. From Radway the ground falls steadily down towards Kineton and a number of drainage ditches join to form streams as they flow down to the river Dene. The terrain may have been altered by a military railway and depot built in 1942, but earlier maps show a tongue of land at around 300 feet above sea level, which extends out towards Kineton, falling sharply to give the effect of a hill from that side. From the Radway side this area is also rising ground, although only by a few feet.

Essex made the best of what was available to him and placed his Foot regiments on the rising ground, described as 'a little round rising hill',

The view from the Castle Inn, high on Edgehill. Military storage bunkers now occupy the ground where Essex deployed his army. The furrows in the centre field show how the ground rises up towards Essex's position.

A gentleman circa 1641. Officers did not wear a uniform and this engraving provides a useful illustration of the appearance of an officer serving on either side. Detail from an engraving by Wenceslaus Hollar.

with Ramsey's left-wing Horse on a small hill fronted by a stream. Both flanks were covered by small fields surrounded by hedges which were occupied by Parliamentarian Dragoons or musketeers. Essex's right wing was more enclosed and the ground in front of his line was rough and crossed by ditches. At least some of the open field in front of Essex's Foot had been ploughed as this was seen to prevent the Royalist cannon fire from ricocheting, and did much to lessen his casualties.

For the Royalists the decision to descend from Edgehill into the plain below represented a risk for if defeated they would have difficulty in making an orderly withdrawal back up the steep slope of the hill. Bulstrode describes the difficulties of the descent of the hill: 'The Foot getting down several Ways which the Horse could not do, by reason of the Hill's Steepness … it was resolved, that Collonel Washington, with his Regiment of Dragoons, should descend the Hill, and possess some Inclosures and Briars on the right Hand of our Army, and a forlorn Hope of Six Hundred Horse were ordered likewise to descend before the Army, and the Carriage Horses of the Cannon were put behind the Carriages, excepting a Horse or two before, and the Foot were ordered to descend as well as they could.'

John Belasyse, whose memoirs were related by his secretary, described how the Royalist Foot were: 'divided into nine bodies, vitz.: five in front and four in reserve, which in the whole consisted of about

The north-east end of Edgehill, known as Knowle End, seen from behind the position taken by the King's Lifeguard of Horse. The ploughed field was also a feature of the battlefield in October 1642.

12,000. The right wing of horse was led by Prince Rupert, the General, and the left by my Lord Willmott, their Lieutenant-General, they being equally divided, about 1,200 in either wing. The King at the head of his Guards disposed himself as he saw occasion; before every body of foot were placed two pieces of cannon, and before them the dragoons, and 1,200 commanded musqueteers as Enfants Perdu.' [Joshua Moone – *A Briefe Relation of the Life and Memoirs of John Lord Belasyse* Part III, HMC Ormonde Mss, Oxford, 1894]

The Royalist field word was 'For God and King Charles'. Bulstrode describes how the King reviewed his troops, and how he was persuaded to retire from the greatest danger. It seems that the King well understood that the coming battle could see the collapse of his cause and was eager to share the dangers with his soldiers. 'The King was that Day in a black Velvet Coat lin'd with Ermin, and a Steel Cap covered with Velvet. He rode to every Brigade of Horse, and to all the Tertia's of Foot, to encourage them to their Duty, being accompanied by the great Officers of the Army; His Majesty spoke to them with great Courage and Chearfulness, which caused Huzza's thro' the whole Army.

'When our Army was drawn up at the Foot of the Hill, and ready to march, all the Generals went to the King (who intended to march with the Army) and desired he would retire to a rising Ground, some Distance from thence, on the Right … from whence he might see the Issue of the Battle, and be out of Danger, and that otherwise the Army would not advance towards the Enemy: To which the King (very unwillingly) was at last perswaded.'

The battle began with a cannonade. Some accounts say the battle began at three o'clock and others at two. The Parliamentarian cavalryman Ludlow says the exchange of cannon fire lasted for an hour, so firing may have begun at two and the engagement of the armies at three. 'The best of our field-pieces were planted upon our right wing, guarded by two regiments of foot, and some horse. Our general having commanded to fire upon the enemy, it was done twice upon that part of the army wherein, as it was reported, the King was. The great shot was exchanged on both sides for the space of an hour or thereabouts.' [*Memoirs of Edmund Ludlow* Part III Oxford 1894]

The Parliamentarian pamphlet *A true copy of a letter sent unto the Right honourable Lord Maior of London from a trusty Friend in the army ...* which was written on 24 October says: 'The ordinance played one upon the other all the time, wee gave them two shoots for one, and their ordinance blessed be the God of battles, did us scarcely any hurt at all whereas we scarcely discharged away a bullet in vaine.'

Other fighting took place as the Dragoons of both armies and groups of 1,200 commanded musketeers on the Royalist side and some of the 700 detached musketeers from the Parliamentarian army fought for possession of the hedges as related in the Royalist official account: 'The Rebels had placed some Musqueteers under a Hedge that crost the Field, where the Encounter was to be made, that flanked upon their left Wing, there were some of the King's Dragooners sent to beat them off, which they very well performed; whereupon our whole Army advanced in very good Order, the Ordnance of both sides playing very fast.' The Parliamentary Dragoons and musketeers came off worst from the fighting and the Royalists had cleared the way for their attack.

THE BATTLE

The battle proper began with the charge of the Royalist Horse on both wings. Prince Rupert had taken care that all the Horse should follow the tactics which had proven so successful at Powick Bridge. The Parliamentarians had not had an opportunity to review their cavalry tactics and as at Powick Bridge they intended to meet the Royalist charge at the halt and to deliver a volley of carbine and pistol shot.

Sir James Ramsey, an experienced Scottish professional soldier, who commanded the Parliamentarian Horse on the left wing, drew on all the stratagems that military science offered to a commander of Horse to strengthen a defensive position. Commanded musketeers had been drawn from the regiments of Holles and Ballard. Three hundred were placed in bodies amongst the squadrons so that the firepower of their muskets could bolster that of the horsemen's carbines. Other musketeers were placed in the hedges to fire into the flanks of the Royalists as they advanced. Finally three cannon were placed to support the Horse.

Ramsey's careful preparations began to unravel when his commanded musketeers were pushed back from their positions in the hedges by Royalist Dragoons. The first of his defences had been undone

An harquebusier firing from the saddle. Dutch cavalry used this as a defensive tactic and Sir James Ramsey's Parliament cavalry attempted, unsuccesfully, to use it at Edgehill. By 1642 an English harquebusier carried pistols with shorter barrels and a helmet with a neck-guard.

and the carefully positioned cannon were no more successful as Bulstrode relates: 'When we came within Cannon Shot of the Enemy, they discharged at us three Pieces of Cannon from their left Wing, commanded by Sir James Ramsey; which Cannon mounted over our Troops, without doing any Hurt, except that their second Shot killed a Quarter-Master in the Rear of the Duke of York's Troop.'

With his flanking force dislodged and his cannon ineffective, Ramsey relied upon the firepower of his horsemen and the musketeers amongst them. Lord Bernard Stuart, who served in the King's Lifeguard of Horse on the extreme right of the cavalry wing gives another view of the charge: 'Upon our approach they gave fire with their cannon lined amongst their horse, dragoneers, carabines and pistols, but finding that did nothing dismay the King's horse and that they came more roundly to them with all their fire reserved, just when our men charged they all began to turn head and we followed an execution upon them for 4 miles together.' [B.M. Harl Ms 3783 fol 60]

It had not been intended that the King's Lifeguard of Horse should take part in the charge as its proper station was in reserve guarding the King. Sir Philip Warwick relates how this came about: 'The King had given leave unto his own Volunteer-Guard of Noblemen and Gentlemen, who with their attendance made two such Troops, as that they consisted of about three hundred Horse: for a vanity had possest that Troop, (upon a little provocation, or for a word of distaste the day before, or being called, *The Troop of Shew*) to desire this honour of being engaged in the first charge'. [*Memoirs of the Reign of King Charles I* Part III, 1702]

This body of 300 Horse could have changed the course of the battle, and of the war, had they remained in reserve and been available to support the Royalist Foot. As it was the Royalist Horse front line was extended to give the King's Lifeguard of Horse its due position on the right of the line and this placed them beyond the open ground where the rest of the Horse had formed up. Consequently the Lifeguard found themselves faced with hedges to jump and the fire of musketeers to endure, although this seems to have had little effect.

One more advantage was to present itself to Rupert. Sir Faithful Fortesque had raised a troop of Horse to join the army to be sent to put down the Irish rebellion and along with other units it had been co-opted into Essex's army. Ready to fight Catholic rebels, Fortesque and his men were not prepared to fight against their King. Many people, both soldiers and civilians, quietly slipped away to change sides during the war, but Fortesque had a more dramatic gesture in mind and sent an officer to inform Rupert that his men would change sides at the moment the Prince made his charge as is told in Prince Rupert's Diary: 'Van Girish Lieutenant to Sir Faithfull Fortesque came over to the Prince, and told him his Captain resolv'd to yield; and that the signall should be the

The personal cavalry standard of the Parliament cavalry commander, the Earl of Bedford. The other Parliament standard was not carried at Edgehill. (Dr Williams Library)

The view south-west from the Castle Inn shows a field pattern, with hedges, briars and open gaps in field boundaries, which may resemble that which made this area difficult for Wilmot's Horse.

shooting off his pistol to the Ground. The time was so short, the Prince could not send notice of it to the Lord Birons, and Sir William Killigrews Troops. By which meanes sevll of them were hurt; by Sir William Killigrews men.'

Despite all his preparations Ramsey's horsemen buckled under the strain of seeing a mass of enemy cavalry heading towards them. They knew they faced Prince Rupert and the Royalist Horse, who had beaten them or their comrades at Powick Bridge. They had seen their supporting musketeers beaten back from the flanking hedges leaving their own flank vulnerable to Royalist Dragoons. They were expected to stand still as the enemy charged towards them and place their faith in a volley of shot to stop the enemy – which it singularly failed to do. Added to all this many would have witnessed one of their own troops fire its pistols into the ground and ride to join the enemy. Faced with the failure of their stand and fire tactics and perhaps believing that others might change sides at any moment it is understandable that the Parliamentarian left wing collapsed as a fighting force. The Horse fled back towards Kineton, joined by many in Charles Essex's infantry brigade, who saw the detached musketeer bodies cut down by the Royalists. Ramsey, with his entire command dispersed, concluded that the situation was beyond his control and as a mercenary rode for London with all speed spreading word of a catastrophic defeat.

The Parliamentarian Officers' account did not attempt to disguise the extent of the débâcle: 'Our Left Wing of Horse, advanced a little forward to the Top of a Hill, where they stood in a Battalia, lined with commanded Musqueteers, 400 out of Col. *Hollis's* Regiment, and 300 out of Col. *Ballard's*; but upon the first Charge of the Enemy, they wheeled about, abandoned their Musqueteers, and came running down with the Enemies Horse at their Heels, and amongst them pellmell, just upon

PRINCE RUPERT'S CHARGE

Prince Rupert, the King's nephew, commanded the Royalist cavalry at Edgehill. Only 22, Rupert had little battlefield experience, but he was one of the most charismatic leaders of the Civil War and managed to create a sense of purpose and enthusiasm amongst the inexperienced cavalrymen who had joined the King's army. His cavalry was formed up three deep in the Swedish style with the best equipped troopers in the front rank. Prince Rupert personally led the Royalist right-wing cavalry and his charge swept away the cavalry on the Parliamentarian army's left wing, commanded by Sir James Ramsey. However, their impetuous pursuit of the fleeing Parliamentarians effectively removed them from the battle.

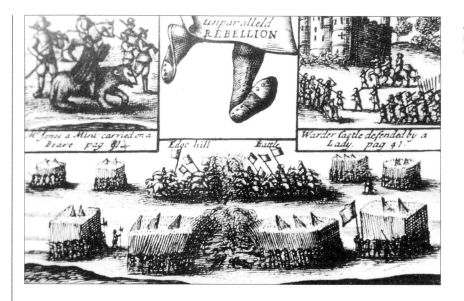

Col. *Hollis's* Regiment, and brake through it, though Col. *Hollis* himself, when he saw them come running towards him, went and planted himself just in the way, and did what possibly he could do to make them stand; and at last prevailed with three Troops to wheel a little about, and rally; but the rest of our Horse of that Wing, and the Enemies Horse with them, brake through and ran to *Keynton* where most of the Enemy left pursuing them, and fell to plundering our Wagons, by which many of us have received very great loss.' Holles's Regiment had stood in the second line of the Parliamentary Foot as part of Ballard's Brigade. Despite the confusion which surrounded them the Londoners stood firm around their Colonel.

At the same time as Rupert launched the right wing of the Royalist Horse into the attack, the left also charged: 'The left wing commanded by Mr, Wilmott, had as good success, though they were to charge in worse ground, amongst hedges, and through gaps and ditches, which were lined with musketeers. But Sir Arthur Aston, with great courage and dexterity, beat off those musketeers with his dragoons; and then the right wing of their horse was as easily routed and dispersed as their left.' [Clarendon]

Essex now faced the loss of both his cavalry wings. Sir William Balfour, another Scots professional, who commanded the Horse on the Parliamentary right wing, was made of sterner stuff than Ramsey. Balfour had placed a formation of Horse in the centre of the army behind the first line of Foot and he now set off to take command of it with a view to seeing what could be saved from the disaster.

To almost all who had witnessed the progress of the battle it seemed that the day was won for the King. However, having charged with great dash and determination the front lines of both Royalist cavalry wings had failed to rally. The second lines were intended as a reserve, to support the first line should its charge fail to break the enemy Horse, or to exploit its success by falling on the exposed flanks of the enemy Foot regiments. Now at the moment when victory was at hand these second line Horse lost their heads and rushed to join the pursuit of the fleeing Parliamentarians. George Digby, who commanded the Royalist second

William Fiennes, Lord Saye and Sele, Colonel of a regiment of Parliament infantry. A leading political figure, he was not with his regiment at Edgehill.

line of Horse on the left flank, had no military experience and afterward maintained that he had never been told that his force was to act as a reserve, but rather to support the first line. That he failed to stop his men joining in the pursuit can be more readily excused when it is remembered that the experienced soldier Sir John Byron, who commanded his own regiment as the second line Horse on the right flank, had no more success in controlling his men. The Royalist Horse had won a great victory in the opening minutes of the battle but they had removed themselves from the field as effectively as if they had been defeated.

THE FOOT ADVANCE

'Sir Jacob Astley … was major Generall of the Army … who, before the charge at the battell at Edge-hill, made a most excellent, pious short and soldierly prayer: for he lifted up his eyes and hands to heaven, saying, *O Lord! thou knowest, how busy I must be this day: if I forget thee, do not thou forget me.* And with that, rose up, crying out, *March on Boys!*' [Sir Philip Warwick]

As the Royalist Foot advanced their reserve brigades commanded by Sir Nicholas Byron and John Belasyse were brought forward to fill the gaps which had been left for them between the front line brigades, so producing a single battle line. From the left of the Royalist line the brigades were now those of Henry Wentworth, Sir Nicholas Byron, Richard Feilding, John Belasyse and Charles Gerard.

The front line Foot regiments of both armies had seen the results of the cavalry battles and some of the Parliamentarian Foot had joined the rout. The brigades of Meldrum on the right and Charles Essex on the

Several enterprising booksellers produced copies of basic infantry training instructions during 1642. These illustrations are based on a much earlier drill manual and show a costume in fashion fifty years earlier.

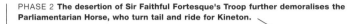

PHASE 2 The desertion of Sir Faithful Fortesque's Troop further demoralises the Parliamentarian Horse, who turn tail and ride for Kineton.

PHASE 5 The entire left side of the Parliamentarian first line has routed. Ballard's and Holles's Regiments (the latter having stood their ground despite being ridden over by Royalist Horse) march up the hill to re-establish the Parliamentarian first line.

PHASE 4 Charles Essex's Parliamentarian Foot brigade rout in the face of the approaching Royalist Horse.

PHASE 4 On the right wing Sir William Fairfax's Regiment, in the second line, also runs.

ESSEX

KINETON

KINETON

PLOUGHED FIEL

PHASE 1 The Dragoons and commanded musketeers contest the hedges and enclosures on each flank of the main battlefield. The Parliamentarians are driven back and the benefit of their flanking fire is lost to their Horse. An hour-long exchange of cannon fire does little harm.

PARLIAMENTARIANS

The right-wing Horse – commanded by the Earl of Bedford (effective commander Sir William Balfour)
1 The Lord General's Regiment
2 Sir William Balfour's Regiment
3 Lord Fielding's Regiment
4 Colonel John Browne's Dragoons, Colonel James Wardlawe's Dragoons

Detached troops of Horse
5 Sir Philip Stapleton's troop of cuirassiers (Lord General's Lifeguard), Captain Nathaniel Draper's troop of harquebusiers
6 Sir William Balfour's troop of cuirassiers, The Earl of Bedford's troop of cuirassiers

The left-wing Horse – commanded by Sir James Ramsey
7 24 troops of Horse and 400 commanded musketeers amongst the Horse
8 300 commanded musketeers in the hedges

THE FOOT

Vanguard
Sir John Meldrum's Brigade (9-12)
9 Sir John Meldrum/Lord Saye & Sele's Regiment
10 Lord Robartes' Regiment
11 Sir William Constable's Regiment
12 Sir William Fairfax's Regiment

Battel
Charles Essex's Brigade (13-16)
13 Charles Essex's Regiment
14 Sir Henry Cholmley's Regiment
15 Lord Mandeville's Regiment or Lord Wharton's Regiment
16 Lord Wharton's Regiment or Lord Mandeville's Regiment

Reereguard
Thomas Ballard's Brigade (17-21)
17 The Lord General's Regiment (Grand Division 1)
18 The Lord General's Regiment (Grand Division 2)
19 Lord Brooke's Regiment
20 Thomas Ballard's Regiment
21 Denzil Holles's Regiment

THE BATTLE OF EDGEHILL

23 October 1642, c. 3.00pm, viewed from the south showing the initial dispositions of the armies, the charge of the Royalist cavalry and the advance of the Royalist Foot brigades.

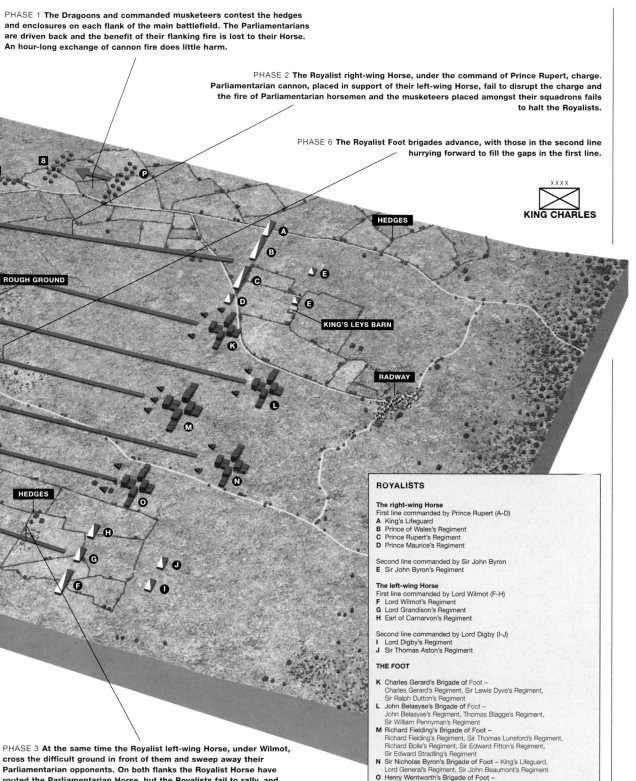

PHASE 1 The Dragoons and commanded musketeers contest the hedges and enclosures on each flank of the main battlefield. The Parliamentarians are driven back and the benefit of their flanking fire is lost to their Horse. An hour-long exchange of cannon fire does little harm.

PHASE 2 The Royalist right-wing Horse, under the command of Prince Rupert, charge. Parliamentarian cannon, placed in support of their left-wing Horse, fail to disrupt the charge and the fire of Parliamentarian horsemen and the musketeers placed amongst their squadrons fails to halt the Royalists.

PHASE 6 The Royalist Foot brigades advance, with those in the second line hurrying forward to fill the gaps in the first line.

xxxx

KING CHARLES

HEDGES

ROUGH GROUND

KING'S LEYS BARN

RADWAY

HEDGES

PHASE 3 At the same time the Royalist left-wing Horse, under Wilmot, cross the difficult ground in front of them and sweep away their Parliamentarian opponents. On both flanks the Royalist Horse have routed the Parliamentarian Horse, but the Royalists fail to rally, and continue the chase until pursued and pursuers become engrossed in the sack of Essex's baggage train in and around Kineton.

ROYALISTS

The right-wing Horse
First line commanded by Prince Rupert (A–D)
A King's Lifeguard
B Prince of Wales's Regiment
C Prince Rupert's Regiment
D Prince Maurice's Regiment

Second line commanded by Sir John Byron
E Sir John Byron's Regiment

The left-wing Horse
First line commanded by Lord Wilmot (F–H)
F Lord Wilmot's Regiment
G Lord Grandison's Regiment
H Earl of Carnarvon's Regiment

Second line commanded by Lord Digby (I–J)
I Lord Digby's Regiment
J Sir Thomas Aston's Regiment

THE FOOT

K Charles Gerard's Brigade of Foot –
Charles Gerard's Regiment, Sir Lewis Dyve's Regiment, Sir Ralph Dutton's Regiment
L John Belasyse's Brigade of Foot –
John Belasyse's Regiment, Thomas Blagge's Regiment, Sir William Pennyman's Regiment
M Richard Fielding's Brigade of Foot –
Richard Fielding's Regiment, Sir Thomas Lunsford's Regiment, Richard Bolle's Regiment, Sir Edward Fitton's Regiment, Sir Edward Stradling's Regiment
N Sir Nicholas Byron's Brigade of Foot – King's Lifeguard, Lord General's Regiment, Sir John Beaumont's Regiment
O Henry Wentworth's Brigade of Foot –
Sir Gilbert Gerard's Regiment, Sir Thomas Salusbury's Regiment, Lord Molineux's Regiment

P Colonel James Usher's Dragoons
Q Colonel Edward Grey's Dragoons, Colonel Edmond Duncombe's Dragoons

left made up the Parliamentary front line with Ballard's Brigade forming a second line. Sir William Fairfax's Regiment from Meldrum's Brigade had been placed in the second line and the Lord General's Regiment may have been deployed in two divisions. This allowed each gap between the first line regiments to be covered by a regiment in the second line. Charles Essex's Brigade had turned tail and fled following the defeat of the left-wing Horse, while Sir William Fairfax's Regiment had fled with the right-wing Horse leaving only Sir William himself with some officers and 100 men. Meldrum was now left to face the approaching Royalist Foot and would have been overwhelmed had not Ballard led his men forward to close the gap.

Ballard's Brigade included Holles's Regiment, which had already lost 400 commanded musketeers along with the 300 detached from Ballard's own regiment. Some of these soldiers may have survived as the rush of horsemen passed them and rejoined their regiments, but many more would have been cut down by Rupert's horsemen or have fled to the hedges and ditches which offered the nearest cover. The Parliamentarian Officers' account recorded the bravery of Ballard's men which saved their army from total defeat. 'Notwithstanding [the routing Horse] breaking through Col. Hollis's Regiment, it was not dismaid, but, together with the other Regiments of that Brigade, marched up the Hill, and so made all the haste they could to come to fight, and got the Wind of the Enemy, and came on (if we may say it our selves, but we must do the Soldiers right) most gallantly, and Charged the Enemy, who were then in fight with our Van, and the Right Wing of our Horse.'

BALFOUR'S CHARGE

The Royalists had won the cavalry battles on both flanks but they had not destroyed all of Essex's Horse formations. Some troops of the regiments of Sir William Balfour and the Lord General's Regiment under Sir Philip Stapleton had been positioned behind Meldrum's Foot Brigade. Sir William Balfour, having seen the right wing of the Parliamentary Horse swept away led these Horse against the Royalist Foot. With the King's own Lifeguard of Horse involved in the confusion about Kineton, no Royalist Horse remained to oppose Balfour and Stapleton. The Parliamentarian Officers' account records the attack: 'Their Foot, which appeared to us, divided into nine great Bodies, came up all in Front, and after some playing with the cannon on both sides, that part of it which was on their Left, and towards our Right wing came on very gallantly to the Charge, and were as gallantly received, and Charged by Sir Philip Stapleton and Sir William Balford's Regiment of Horse, assisted with the Lord Robert's, and Sir William Constable's Regiments of Foot, who did it so home thrice together, that they forced all the Musqueteers, of two of their left Regiments, to run in and shrowd themselves within their Pikes, not daring to shoot a shot, and so stood when our Rear came up; and then Charging altogether, especially that part of our Rear which was placed upon the Right hand, and so next unto them which was the Lord General's Regiment, and the Lord Brook's, led on by Col. Ballard who commanded that Brigade, forced that Stand of Pikes, and wholly broke those two regiments, and slew and took almost every man of them.'

Three troops of Horse in the Parliament Army were equipped as cuirassiers. Some individual cavalrymen on both sides, officers and gentlemen volunteers, would also have worn this armour.

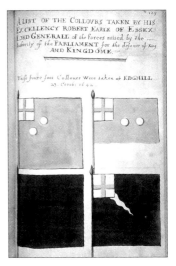

Four Royalist infantry flags captured at Edgehill from a contemporary illustrated 'List of the Collours taken by His Excellency, Robert Earle of Essex Lord Generall'. Source MS Jonathon Turmile. (Dr Williams Library)

Edgehill seen from the viewpoint of the Parliamentary right wing. The Castle Inn is just visible in the centre of the picture. The gentle slope of the plain is clear but the steepness of the ridge is hidden by the trees.

We have no plan of the Parliamentary forces and cannot say where Meldrum's own regiment of Foot stood in the line, but it may have held the post of honour on the right of the line. Next in line were Lord Robartes' and Sir William Constable's regiments who took the brunt of the attack and at this crucial moment in the battle Balfour led his cavalry forward to support them. With no Horse troops of their own to protect them, the three left-hand Royalist Foot brigades were in great peril and resorted to the usual tactical response for Foot attacked by Horse. The pikemen formed a ring or square and the musketeers ran beneath the stand of pikes to seek shelter from the slashing swords of the enemy horsemen. The brigade of Sir Nicholas Byron succeeded in changing into a defensive formation, but Feilding was not so fortunate.

Essex had placed the front line of his army on higher ground, and the Parliamentarian Officers' account makes it clear that Ballard's Brigade was behind a hill and had to march up the reverse slope to reach its new position in the front line. Stapleton and Balfour's Horse troops were also positioned on the reverse slope of the high ground and although they would have been visible to an observer high on Edgehill, such as Bulstrode early in the day, it is unlikely that they would have been visible to an officer on horseback in the Royalist lines. This may explain why their presence was missed by the officers of both Royalist cavalry wings and why their attack came as such a shock to the Royalist Foot brigades.

As Richard Feilding's Brigade of Foot advanced towards Meldrum's Brigade his men must have believed that all the Parliamentarian Horse had been chased from the field. The sudden appearance of heavily armoured cuirassier troopers rising as if from the earth in the gaps between Lord Robartes'and Constable's regiments of Foot and falling on

65

'ASTLEY'S PRAYER'
THE ROYALIST INFANTRY PREPARE TO ADVANCE
Sir Jacob Astley commanded the Royalist infantry at Edgehill. When he heard the signal to advance, perhaps the first shots from the Royalist artillery, Astley 'made a most excellent, pious, short and soldierly prayer: for he lifted up his hands and eyes to Heaven, saying *O, Lord! Thou knowest how busy I must be this day: If I forget thee, do not thou forget me*. And with that he rose up crying out, *March on Boys!*' Then he led the whole of the Royalist infantry forward and they 'came on very gallantly to the Charge'.

Sir Charles Lucas,
Lieutenant-Colonel of the
Earl of Carnarvon's regiment
of Royalist cavalry at Edgehill.
Lucas was a professional
officer who had served in the
Dutch Army.

the flanks of their battalions, would have come as a terrible shock to the untried recruits. Unfamiliar with their Swedish brigade formations Feilding's regiments were cut down piecemeal with the loss of Feilding himself as a prisoner along with Colonels Lunsford and Stradling from his brigade, which leaderless fled back towards Edgehill.

The Royalists now faced a combined attack of Horse and Foot as the Parliamentarian musketeers poured shot into their close-packed ranks. The King's musketeers were unable to load their muskets to return fire as they crouched under the pikes and the steadily approaching Parliamentary pike blocks threatened to trap them against their own pikemen while unable to defend themselves. At this decisive moment the regiments of the Earl of Essex and Lord Brooke were brought up from the Parliamentary second line by Thomas Ballard, their brigade commander. James II gave an account of the fighting: 'The Earle of Essex observing that all the King's horse were gone off in pursuit of his left wing, commanded that part of his cavalery which was behind his foot, to charge the King's and the general's regiments in the flanck, just at the time when they were so warmly ingaged at push of pike with his men. Tis true they were not broken with this charge, yet they were put into some disorder, which the Enemy's foot observing, advanced upon them, and drove them back as far as to their cannon.' [*Life of James II* Part III, 1816]

Sir William Balfour and his troops of Horse followed up their success by reaching the Royalist artillery. The Parliamentary Officers' account says: 'Sir William Balfour, who in the beginning of the Day broke a Regiment of Foot which had green Colours, beat them to their Cannon, where they threw down their Arms, and ran away; he laid his hand upon the Cannon, and called for Nails to nail them up, especially the two biggest, which were Demy-Cannon; but finding none, he cut the ropes belonging to them, and his Troopers killed the Canoneers; then he pursued the Fliers half a Mile upon Execution.'

Balfour's Horse burst through the Royalist battle line and cut about them as they chased the fleeing Royalists back towards the slopes of Edgehill. Falling on a battery of the King's guns Balfour wished to hammer nails into the touchholes of the cannon so as to render them useless. Removing these nails from a muzzle-loading cannon would only have been possible by drilling out the nail, not a task which could be accomplished on the field of battle. None of the Parliamentarian troopers had been equipped with such nails and Balfour had to make do with the next best option of cutting the ropes by which the guns were drawn, making it difficult for the Royalists to remove them from the battlefield.

Although they were not aware of it at the time a party of Balfour's Horse had come close to capturing the young Prince Charles and his brother James, Duke of York: 'Sr. Will. Howard went off with the Prince and Duke pursuant to his orders. and they had not gone above musket shott of from the place, when they saw a body of horse advancing directly towards them from the left hand of the King's foot; upon which sending to see what they were, and finding them to be the Enemy, they drew behind a little barn not far distant from them, which was incompassed by a hedge. In this barn severall of the King's wounded men were then dressing, but the Enemy observing the King's men to be within the inclosure, drew immediately back without ingaging them, by which means the Prince and the Duke escaped the evident danger of being taken; for had they charged that small party they could not have fail'd of beating them, considering the vast advantage of their numbers.' [James II]

Ludlow, who served in Essex's Lifeguard under Sir Philip Stapleton, describes an instance of friendly fire upon Balfour's returning troops: 'We perceived that those who were appointed to guard the artillery were marched off; and Sir Philip Stapylton, our captain, wishing for a regiment of foot to secure the cannon, we promised to stand by him in defence of them, causing one of our servants to load and level one of them, which he had scarce done, when a body of horse appeared advancing towards us from that side where the enemy was. We fired at them with case-shot, but did no other mischief save only wounding one man through the hand, our gun being overloaded, and planted on high ground; which fell out very happily, this body of horse being of our own army, and commanded by Sir William Balfour, who with great resolution had charged into the enemy's quarters, where he had nailed several pieces of their cannon, and was then retreating to his own party, of which the man who was shot in the hand was giving us notice by holding it up; but we did not discern it.'

STAPLETON'S CHARGE

Balfour's charge had broken through the enemy's centre and routed Feilding's Brigade. On the Royalist left the pikemen of Sir Nicholas Byron had been able to hold off the Parliamentary Horse commanded by Sir Philip Stapleton. Ludlow identifies the body which Stapleton's Horse attacked by his mention of the Royal Standard which was with Sir Nicholas Byron's Brigade of Royalist Foot. As previously described the Royalist musketeers took cover below their regiment's pike bodies into which the Parliamentary Horse was unable to break: 'The enemy's body of foot, wherein the King's standard was, came on within musket-shot of us; upon which we observing no horse to encounter withal, charged then with some loss from their pikes, tho very little from their shot; but not being able to break them, we retreated to our former station.' [Ludlow]

The Earl of Essex, who is reported to have fought with his own regiment of Foot, pike in hand, now ordered his own regiment of Foot and that of Lord Brooke forward to support Stapleton's Horse attack on their flank. Against this assault on front and flank by combined arms of Horse and Foot the Royalist Foot held firm, but when assailed in the rear by Balfour's Horse returning from their charge, they crumpled and fell back in confusion as Ludlow describes: 'The Earl of Essex order'd two regiments of foot to attack that body which we had charged before, where the King's standard was, which they did, but could not break them till Sir William Balfour at the head of a party of horse charging them in the rear, and we marching down to take them in the flank, they brake and ran away towards the hill.'

The King's Lifeguard of Foot lost 11 of its 13 colours in this rout and both Byron and the Earl of Lindsey were wounded. The Royalist brigade of Henry Wentworth did not press home its attack on Meldrum's Regiment and may have now withdrawn for Clarendon remarks that at the battle of Brentford, later in the campaign, the Welsh soldiers of Sir

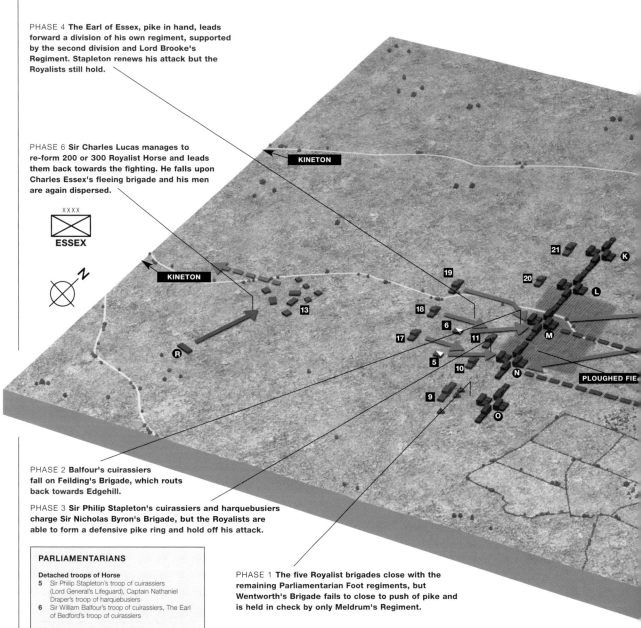

PHASE 4 **The Earl of Essex, pike in hand, leads forward a division of his own regiment, supported by the second division and Lord Brooke's Regiment. Stapleton renews his attack but the Royalists still hold.**

PHASE 6 **Sir Charles Lucas manages to re-form 200 or 300 Royalist Horse and leads them back towards the fighting. He falls upon Charles Essex's fleeing brigade and his men are again dispersed.**

ESSEX

KINETON

KINETON

KINETON

PLOUGHED FIE

PHASE 2 **Balfour's cuirassiers fall on Feilding's Brigade, which routs back towards Edgehill.**

PHASE 3 **Sir Philip Stapleton's cuirassiers and harquebusiers charge Sir Nicholas Byron's Brigade, but the Royalists are able to form a defensive pike ring and hold off his attack.**

PHASE 1 **The five Royalist brigades close with the remaining Parliamentarian Foot regiments, but Wentworth's Brigade fails to close to push of pike and is held in check by only Meldrum's Regiment.**

PARLIAMENTARIANS

Detached troops of Horse
5   Sir Philip Stapleton's troop of cuirassiers
     (Lord General's Lifeguard), Captain Nathaniel
     Draper's troop of harquebusiers
6   Sir William Balfour's troop of cuirassiers, The Earl
     of Bedford's troop of cuirassiers

The Foot

Vanguard – Sir John Meldrum's Brigade (9-11)
9   Sir John Meldrum/Lord Saye & Sele's Regiment
10   Lord Robartes' Regiment
11   Sir William Constable's Regiment

13   **Battel** – Charles Essex's Brigade (remnants)

Rereguard – Thomas Ballard's Brigade (17-21)
17   The Lord General's Regiment (Grand Division 1)
18   The Lord General's Regiment (Grand Division 2)
19   Lord Brooke's Regiment
20   Thomas Ballard's Regiment
21   Denzil Holles's Regiment

THE BATTLE OF EDGEHILL
23 October 1642, c. 3.30–4.30pm, viewed from the south showing the clash of the Royalist and Parliament Foot brigades, and the charge of Balfour's and Stapleton's cuirassier troops.

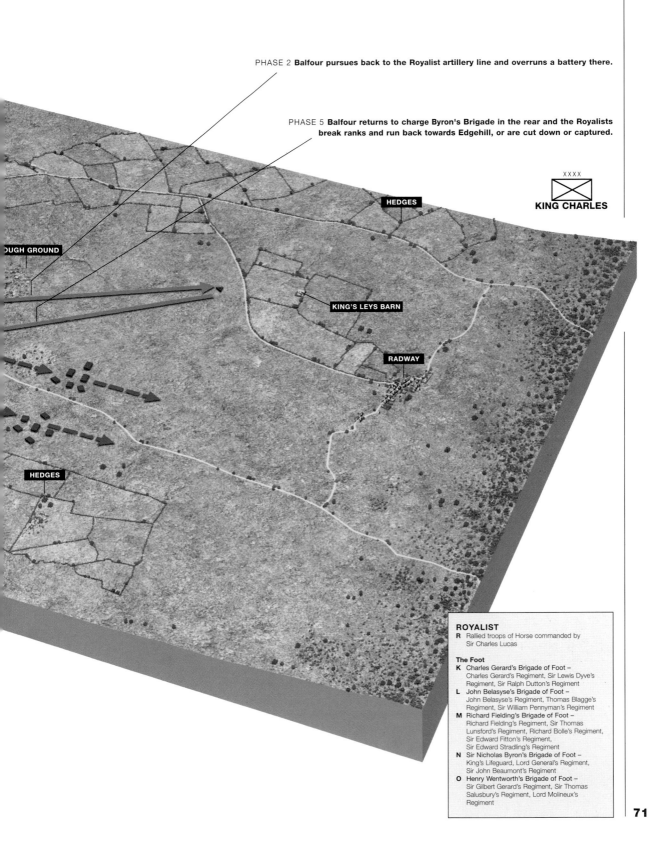

PHASE 2 **Balfour pursues back to the Royalist artillery line and overruns a battery there.**

PHASE 5 **Balfour returns to charge Byron's Brigade in the rear and the Royalists break ranks and run back towards Edgehill, or are cut down or captured.**

XXXX
KING CHARLES

HEDGES

ROUGH GROUND

KING'S LEYS BARN

RADWAY

HEDGES

ROYALIST

R Rallied troops of Horse commanded by
Sir Charles Lucas

The Foot

K Charles Gerard's Brigade of Foot –
Charles Gerard's Regiment, Sir Lewis Dyve's
Regiment, Sir Ralph Dutton's Regiment

L John Belasyse's Brigade of Foot –
John Belasyse's Regiment, Thomas Blagge's
Regiment, Sir William Pennyman's Regiment

M Richard Fielding's Brigade of Foot –
Richard Fielding's Regiment, Sir Thomas
Lunsford's Regiment, Richard Bolle's Regiment,
Sir Edward Fitton's Regiment,
Sir Edward Stradling's Regiment

N Sir Nicholas Byron's Brigade of Foot –
King's Lifeguard, Lord General's Regiment,
Sir John Beaumont's Regiment

O Henry Wentworth's Brigade of Foot –
Sir Gilbert Gerard's Regiment, Sir Thomas
Salusbury's Regiment, Lord Molineux's
Regiment

At Ege-hill 16 peeces of Canon shot against 80 of E: of Essex Liffegard & not one man hurte, & those 80 brake in upon 1000 of the Kings. 4 of yᵉ Parlia: Reg: ran away & 16 troops of Horse, so wee wayre 6000 & they 18000, yet wee tooke yᵉ Standard & Clefte Sʳ: Ed: Varney Standerbearer in the head & Slew the Lord Lindsey Generall of the Fielde.

Thomas Salusbury's Regiment recovered their honour having behaved poorly at Edgehill where they had served under Wentworth. The left and centre of the Royalist Foot were now routed or falling back in confusion.

The Royal Standard

The defeat of Sir Nicholas Byron's Brigade had seen the capture by the Parliamentarians of the King's Royal Standard. Sir Edmund Verney was cut down using the Standard as if it were a pike to defend himself: 'He himself killed two with his owne hands … and brocke the poynt of his standard at push of pike before he fell.' [Sir Edward Sydenham's letter to Ralph Verney from *The Standard Bearer* by Major Peter Verney]

The Standard was brought before the Earl of Essex, who entrusted it to a servant to be taken to the rear. Captain John Smith, of Lord Grandison's Regiment of Horse, had taken part in the success of the Royalist Horse on the left wing and had rallied with some 200 horsemen under the command of Sir Charles Lucas. Having charged first the routing soldiers of Charles Essex's Regiment and then those of Lord Wharton's Regiment, Smith found himself with only one follower who had not joined the pursuit. Returning to his own lines he saw 'six men, three Curiasiers and three Harquebusiers on horse-backe, guarding a seventh on foot, who was carrying off the Field Colours rouled up which he conceived to be one of the ordinary Colours of His Majesties Leifeguards, and therefore seeing them so strong, intended to avoide them …' [Edward Walsingham, *Brittannicae Virtutis Imago*, Oxford, 1644]

Smith was told by a boy that the rebels were carrying off the Royal Standard. Smith charged the Parliamentarians and wounded Essex's servant in the breast: 'Whil'st he was bent forward to follow his thrust, one of those Curiasiers with a pollax wounded him in the necke through the Collar of his doublet, and the rest gave fire at him with their pistolls, but without any further hurt then blowing off some pouder into his face.

'No sooner was he recovered upright, but he made a thrust at the Curiasier that wounded him, and ran him in the belly, whereupon he presently fell, at which sight all the rest ran away. Then he caused a foot souldier that was neare at hand to reach him up the banner, which he brought away with the horse of that Curiasier.' [Edward Walsingham]

Not content with this exploit Smith later rescued from his captors Richard Feilding, who had fallen into the hands of ten Parliamentarians when his Foot brigade had been routed. Smith was knighted by the King the following day.

THE FIGHTING
ON THE ROYALIST RIGHT WING

On the right of the Royalist line the two Foot brigades of John Belasyse and Charles Gerard stood firm. The part of the Parliamentary line to which they were opposed had been held by the four regiments of Charles Essex's Brigade, comprising the regiments of Charles Essex himself, Lord Wharton, Lord Mandeville and Sir Henry Cholmley. However, these regiments were now streaming back towards Kineton, having fled at the first charge of Rupert's Horse. To fill the gap Thomas Ballard led forward his brigade of four Foot regiments. From the accounts given above we know that two of these regiments, those of the Earl of Essex (the Lord General's Regiment) and Lord Brooke's, moved forward to oppose the left and centre of the Royalist line. There remained the regiments of Ballard himself and of Denzil Holles, both weakened by the detachment of 700 musketeers who had been lost in the rout following Rupert's charge or were still with the Dragoons on the far left flank. Belasyse was wounded in the action so his brigade must have been heavily involved in the fighting. With Wentworth's Brigade inactive or falling back and Belasyse's suffering casualties, the only body of Foot which remained firm was that of Charles Gerard on the extreme right of the Royalist line. Opposed only by the weakened regiments of Ballard and Holles, Gerard had less to do to hold his place in the line and was able to make a steady withdrawal to cover the retreat of the other Royalist brigades as James II's memoirs recall: 'At the same time the remnant of their foot were pressing vigorously on the King's, and had not the right hand Brigade commanded by Coll. Charles Gerard kept their order, and plyd those regiments which advanced upon them, with so great courage that they put the Enemy to a stand, the whole body of the King's foot had run great hazard of an absolute defeat; for had his Majesty's two wings given way, those in the main-battell could have made no long resistance. After this neither party press'd the other, but contented themselves to keep their ground, and continued fireing, till night put an end to the dispute.'

The Parliamentarian pamphlet *A Most True relation of the Present State of His Maiesties Army*, dated 3 December, says of the Royalist army: 'The King's (upon its rowting) was gladd to steale away; I might say Flye, which they did with clypped wings: For no lesse, then five whole regiments (and those their very best, both for Number of men, and completeness of furniture) by name, the Lord Generall's, Sir Raphe Duttone's, Colonel Blage's, Colonel Bollis's and Sir Lewis Dyve's which though it scaped best, because he, and Captain Slingsby are left alive, all the other foure's Officers being wholly cut of, together with the Souldiers that served under their Command; yet that regiment now hath nothing, but their barelives to boast of.'

'NAILS, NAILS' – BALFOUR OVERRUNS THE ROYALIST CANNON

Sir William Balfour was a Lieutenant General and effective commander of the Parliament cavalry as 'the earl of Bedford had the name of general of the horse, though that command principally depended upon Sir William Balfore'. Balfour deployed some of his best cavalry behind the Parliament infantry lines and they remained in the field when the Royalist cavalry swept away both Parliament cavalry wings and then chased after them. With the only formed cavalry left on the battlefield, Balfour was able to exercise an influence out of all proportion to the actual number of his troopers. He broke a 'Regiment of Foot which had green Colours, beat them to their Cannon, where they threw down their Arms and ran away; he laid his hand upon the Cannon, and called for Nails to nail them up, especially the two biggest, which were Demy-Cannon; but finding none, he cut the ropes belonging to them, and his troopers killed the Canoneers; then he pursued the Fliers half a mile upon Execution'.

Oliver Cromwell. A captain of a troop of Parliament cavalry in 1642, Cromwell and his troop reached Edgehill during the closing stages of the battle.

An example of a lighter matchlock musket, which did not require a musket rest. (By courtesy of the Board of Trustees, Royal Armouries)

Although Parliamentarian propaganda, the pamphlet may truly be the work of a Royalist deserter as no mention is made of regiments the Parliamentarians knew to have been routed at Edgehill. As this is a view of the Royalist Army some days after the battle it may indicate that the casualties and disorder caused to the Royalist brigades at Edgehill was greater, even amongst those which did not rout, than their own accounts admit.

THE BATTLE DRAWS TO A CLOSE

Gerard's men were not left without support for long. At long last some of the Royalist Horse had been brought back under control and returned to save the remnants of their Foot as the Royalist Official account describes: 'By this time the Right Wing of our Horse was returned from Chasing the Rebels, and were in some Confusion, because they Came from the Execution; but seeing our Foot and Cannon in some danger to be lost, by reason that the Rebels Horse and Foot (those Horse which had never been Charged) advanced in good Order to Charge; ours made a stand and soon rallied together, having some Dragoons with them, and so advancing, made the Dragooners give them a Volley or two of Shot, which made the Rebels instantly retire. By this time it was grown so dark, that our Chief Commanders durst not Charge for fear of mistaking Friends for Foes... whereupon both Armies retreated, ours in such Order, that we not only brought off our own Cannon, but 4 of the Rebels, we retiring to the Top of the Hill from whence we came; because of the advantage of the Place, and theirs to the Village where they had been quartere'd the Night before.'

Royalist Horse had been late in making a return to the field of battle. Prince Rupert rallied three to five troops which returned to support the retreating Foot. The Parliamentarian Officers' account records the presence of some Royalist Horse at this time: 'Sir Philip Stapleton, who, when Five Troops of the Enemies Horse returned from pursuit of our Left Wing, and from Plundering some of our Wagons, and passed by the outside of our Rear upon the Left hand, went and Charged them with

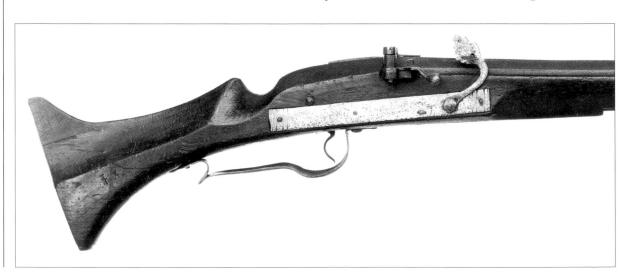

his Troop, and made them run; but they finding a Gap in the Hedge, got away, and returned to the rest of their broken Troops, where they rallied and made up a kind of a Body again.'

Ludlow took part in this action and gives his account of the end of the battle: 'Towards the close of the day we discovered a body of horse marching from our rear on the left of us under the hedges, which the life-guard (whom I had then found) having discovered to be the enemy, and resolving to charge them, sent to some of our troops that stood within musket-shot of us to second them; which though they refused to do, and we had no way to come at them but through a gap in the hedge, we advanced towards them and falling upon their rear, killed divers of them, and brought off some arms. In which attempt being dismounted I could not without great difficulty recover on horse-back again, being loaded with cuirassier's arms, as the rest of the guard also were.'

Lord Falkland, the King's Secretary of State, urged Lord Wilmot to make one last charge with the Horse that had re-formed. He received the reply, 'My Lord, we have got the day, and let us live to enjoy the fruit thereof.' [Clarendon]

As the day wore on other units from Essex's army began to arrive. Between 3.00 and 4.00pm John Fiennes with two troops of Horse arrived from their billets in Evesham. Hamden's and Grantham's regiments, along with nine or ten troops of Horse and six companies of Dragoons encountered Royalist Horse around Kineton and engaged them sufficiently ardently to suffer casualties. They were not able to intervene in the main fighting before dark. As late as Monday morning Lord Rochford's Regiment arrived at the end of a long march from Coventry.

Bulstrode describes the fighting around Kineton and gives a graphic account of the nature of the cavalry hand-to-hand fighting: 'And we of the Prince of Wales's Regiment, (who were all scattered) pursued also, till we met with two Foot Regiments of Hambden and *Hollis*, and with a Regiment of Horse coming from Warwick to their Army, which made us hasten as fast back as we had pursued. In this Pursuit I was wounded in the Head by a Person who turned upon me, and struck me with his Pole-axe, and was seconding his Blow, when Sir Thomas Byron being near, he shot him dead with his Pistol, by which Means I came back.'

On the Royalist side of the field Clarendon records that senior officers advised the King to abandon his cannon and Foot regiments and to march with the Horse to the west. Only resolute opposition by Sir John Culpeper turned the tide of the argument and the King decided to stand his ground and to await events. Bulstrode gives a characteristically frank opinion of the Royalist victory: 'The Night then soon parted both Armies, and both Sides pretended to the Victory; but since we retired up the Hill, from whence we came down, and left the Champ de Battaile to the Enemy, I think we had no great Reason to brag of a Victory; For the King, with a great Part of the Army marched that Night up to Wormington Hills, it being a hard Frost, and very cold. But that which made us think we had the Victory, was that whereas the Earl of Essex was commanded to hinder our getting to London before him, by this Battle we were nearest London, and might have been there much before the Earl of Essex.'

Two Royalist infantry flags (top) captured at Edgehill. The four Royalist cavalry cornets shown were captured at Cirencester in September 1643 but give a good impression of the designs used by Royalist cavalry captains. (Dr Williams Library)

THE CAPTURE OF THE ROYAL STANDARD

The Royal Standard was carried at Edgehill by Sir Edmund Verney, Knight Marshal of the King's Palace. At the outbreak of the Civil War Verney's loyalties were torn between his duty and his conscience, but he wrote that as 'I have eaten his bread and served him near thirty years' he could not 'do so base a Thing as to forsake' his King and 'chuse rather to lose my Life (which I am sure I shall do) to preserve and defend those Things which are against my Conscience to preserve'. At Edgehill he 'nither put on armes [armour] or buffe cote'. As the Royalist infantry at the centre of the battle began to crumble under attack from opposing infantry and cavalry, Verney 'adventured with His Majesty's colours among the enemy so that the soldiers might be encouraged to follow him'. A desperate fight developed around the standard and Verney was cut down by a 'Gentleman of the Lord General's Troops of Horse' as he used the standard as a pike. Sir Edmund's body was never found, only his hand hacked off as it grasped the standard pole. A ring with a miniature portrait of Charles I identified the hand and was returned to his family.

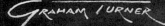

AFTERMATH

The day following the battle

Those soldiers who had not slipped away in search of warmth and food spent a cold and hungry night, the Parliamentarians on the battlefield and the Royalists on the exposed slopes and plateau of Edgehill. The Royalist official account tells what happened the next morning: 'The King with the whole Body of the Horse, and those of the Foot which were not broken, quartered upon and on one side of the Hill, all that Night; and in the Morning, as soon as it was Day, drew half the Body of the Horse into Battalia, at the Foot of the Hill, and the rest of the Horse and the Foot on the Top of the Hill, where the Standard was placed; and having notice that 3 of the Rebels Cannon were left half way between us and their Quarter, sent out a Body of Horse, and drew them off; they not so much as offering to relieve them.

'So both Armies, facing one another all day, retired at Night to their former Quarters.'

The Parliamentarians made better use of the respite offered by darkness and slipped back to Kineton to their old quarters as the Parliamentary Officers' account tells: 'We stood in very good Order; drew up all our Forces, both Horse and Foot; and so stood all that Night upon the place where the Enemy, before the Fight, had drawn into Battalia, till toward Morning, that the Enemy was gone, and retired up the Hill, and then we returned also to a warmer place near Keynton, where we had Quarter the Night before; for we were almost starved with cold that bitter Night, our Army being in extream want of Victuals; and about 9 or 10 of the Clock drew out again into Battalia, and so stood 3 or 4 hours, till the Enemy was clean gone from the Hill, and then we drew again into our Quarter, and there have lain this Night, and purpose this Day, (God willing) after we have buried our Dead, to march to Warwick to refresh our Army.'

The following day many in both armies expected that the battle would be resumed and on both sides a speedy victory was expected. The Royalist Foot had been badly mauled in the battle and had shown that their tactics, training and equipment were not sufficient to stand up to an enemy reinforced by fresh regiments. The King's Horse remained dispersed and those that had regrouped could not attack the Parliamentary army alone. The Parliamentarian force had been reinforced by two of the best regiments of Foot in their army and some ten troops of Horse as well as their train of heavy artillery, but their main strength of Horse had been routed in the battle and they could do little without them. Both sides complained of a lack of ammunition and powder towards the end of the battle. The Parliamentary train brought up their reserves of powder and ammunition, but the King may not have enjoyed a similar advantage.

On the Tuesday, the second day after the battle, as related above, Essex withdrew his army to Warwick, but Prince Rupert did not let him go unmolested as Bulstrode relates: 'We rested all Monday upon the Hill, to put our Army in Order; and seeing the Enemy (as we thought) were preparing to retire, Prince Rupert was resolved, that Monday Night, to go down the Hill, at a Place called Sun-Rising, a Mile on our left Hand, and to fall upon the Enemy in their Retreat; and on Tuesday Morning very early, the Prince, with a strong Detachment of Horse and Dragoons, fell into Keinton, where he found all Houses full of wounded and sick Men, with divers Officers, and several Waggons loaded with Muskets and Pikes, and all Sorts of Ammunition, preparing to follow the Army, which was marched towards Warwick.'

Edgehill to the south of the battlefield by Sun Rising, from where Prince Rupert launched his cavalry raid on Kineton two days after the battle. The sparse scrub bushes give some idea of how Edgehill appeared in 1642.

The performance of the commanders and their armies

The Earl of Essex deployed his men in a modern formation, using a model which combined the latest styles to come out of the Thirty Years War with a depth of deployment – eight deep for his infantry and six for his cavalry – which suited the Dutch-style training and experience of the majority of his officers and men. His cavalry fled in the face of Royalist cavalry charges and one of his infantry brigades had followed them. His survival had depended upon the courage and determination of the remainder of his infantry and the success of his tactic in deploying some of his best cavalry amongst them. The essential combination of brave men and effective tactics.

Prince Rupert had deployed his men in a model that copied the infantry deployment of Gustavus Adolphus, but by 1642 this had not been used in western Europe for eight years and was not the latest European style. Prince Rupert had little practical experience in warfare

PARLIAMENTARIANS

Detached troops of Horse

5   Sir Philip Stapleton's troop of cuirassiers
    (Lord General's Lifeguard), Captain Nathaniel
    Draper's troop of harquebusiers
6   Sir William Balfour's troop of cuirassiers, The
    Earl of Bedford's troop of cuirassiers

The Foot
Vanguard
Sir John Meldrum's Brigade (9-11)
9   Sir John Meldrum/Lord Saye & Sele's Regiment
10 Lord Robartes' Regiment
11 Sir William Constable's Regiment

Rereguard
Thomas Ballard's Brigade (17-21)
17 The Lord General's Regiment (Grand Division 1)
18 The Lord General's Regiment (Grand Division 2)
19 Lord Brooke's Regiment
20 Thomas Ballard's Regiment
21 Denzil Holles's Regiment

22 Hamden's and Grantham's Regiments of Foot
    with supporting Horse and Dragoons

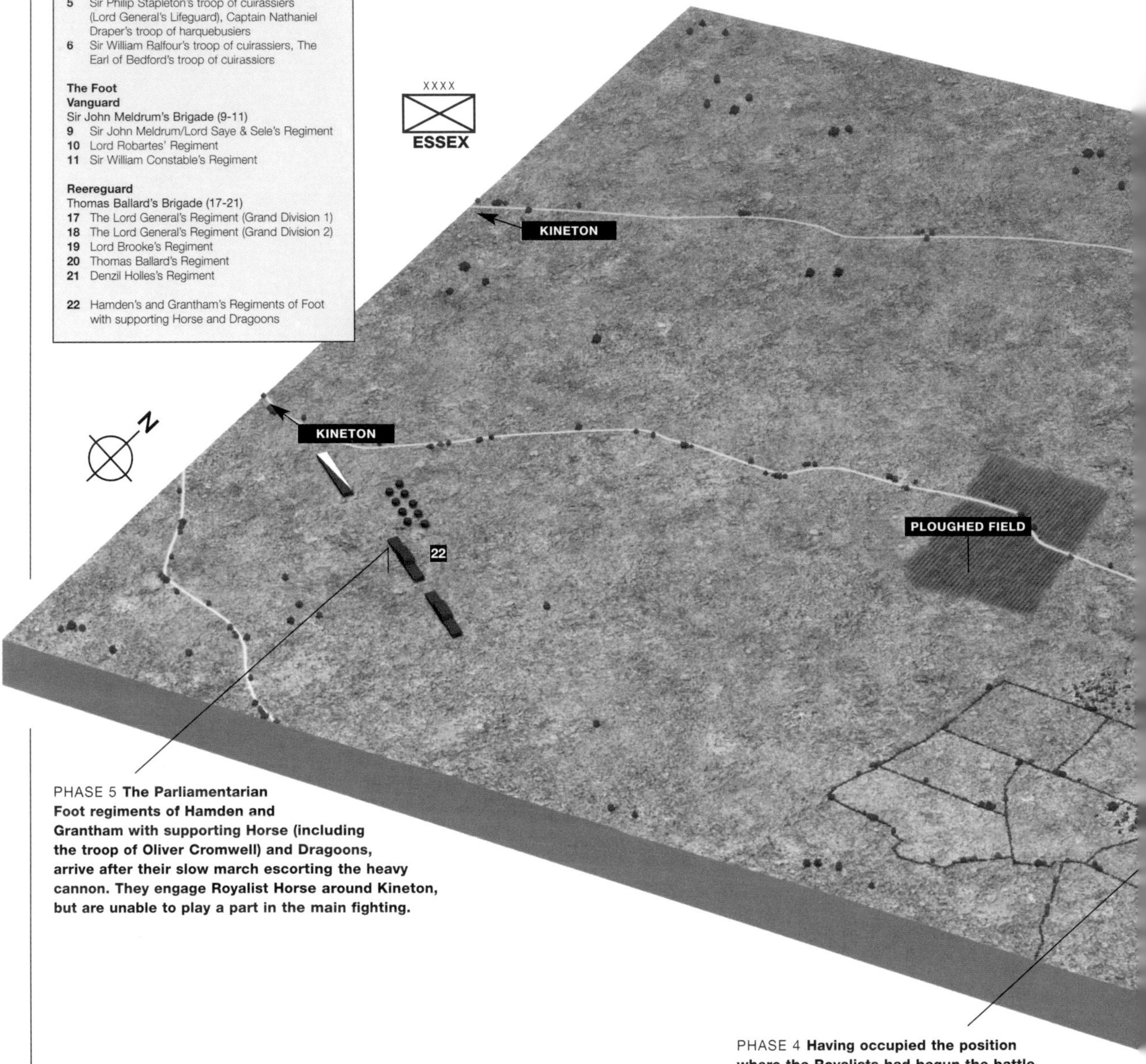

ESSEX

KINETON

KINETON

PLOUGHED FIELD

22

PHASE 5 **The Parliamentarian
Foot regiments of Hamden and
Grantham with supporting Horse (including
the troop of Oliver Cromwell) and Dragoons,
arrive after their slow march escorting the heavy
cannon. They engage Royalist Horse around Kineton,
but are unable to play a part in the main fighting.**

PHASE 4 **Having occupied the position
where the Royalists had begun the battle,
the Parliamentarians, short of powder and
ammunition, are content to hold their
position.**

THE BATTLE OF EDGEHILL

23 October 1642, c.4.30–6.00pm, viewed from the south showing the closing stages of the battle. With
two of their five infantry brigades routed the Royalists fall back as best they can to positions behind those
from which they began the battle. Having lost a large part of their army, including almost all the cavalry,
the Parliamentarians are in a poor state to exploit their success against the Royalist infantry

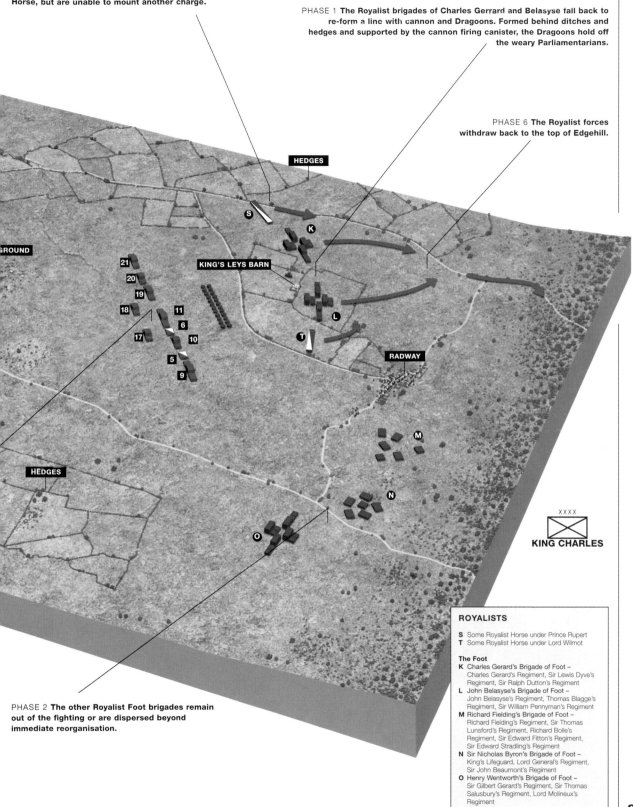

PHASE 3 **Prince Rupert and Wilmot return with some Royalist Horse, but are unable to mount another charge.**

PHASE 1 **The Royalist brigades of Charles Gerrard and Belasyse fall back to re-form a line with cannon and Dragoons. Formed behind ditches and hedges and supported by the cannon firing canister, the Dragoons hold off the weary Parliamentarians.**

PHASE 6 **The Royalist forces withdraw back to the top of Edgehill.**

HEDGES

GROUND

KING'S LEYS BARN

RADWAY

HEDGES

PHASE 2 **The other Royalist Foot brigades remain out of the fighting or are dispersed beyond immediate reorganisation.**

XXXX

KING CHARLES

ROYALISTS

S Some Royalist Horse under Prince Rupert
T Some Royalist Horse under Lord Wilmot

The Foot
K Charles Gerard's Brigade of Foot –
Charles Gerard's Regiment, Sir Lewis Dyve's Regiment, Sir Ralph Dutton's Regiment
L John Belasyse's Brigade of Foot –
John Belasyse's Regiment, Thomas Blagge's Regiment, Sir William Pennyman's Regiment
M Richard Fielding's Brigade of Foot –
Richard Fielding's Regiment, Sir Thomas Lunsford's Regiment, Richard Bolle's Regiment, Sir Edward Fitton's Regiment, Sir Edward Stradling's Regiment
N Sir Nicholas Byron's Brigade of Foot –
King's Lifeguard, Lord General's Regiment, Sir John Beaumont's Regiment
O Henry Wentworth's Brigade of Foot –
Sir Gilbert Gerard's Regiment, Sir Thomas Salusbury's Regiment, Lord Molineux's Regiment

83

although he had a thorough understanding of the theory. He sought to win the war in one massive fast-moving attack with both cavalry and infantry. His cavalry lost the advantage of a reserve as its second line supports followed the first lines in pursuit and his infantry attacked on a single front without a reserve, a gamble in tactics which aimed at complete victory but lacked depth if checked.

The casualties

Of the men who fought that day, some fought like heroes, some ran. The details of wounded Parliament soldiers show that those regiments which fought hard lost heavily but those who fled suffered as badly, as fleeing men were cut down by Royalist cavalry as they ran. Ludlow recorded: 'It was observed that the greatest slaughter on our side was of such as ran

Parliament Casualties from Edgehill

Details survive of the disbursement of funds provided for wounded Parliament soldiers by Lord Brooke for those carried to Warwick and the Earl of Essex for wounded men carried to Coventry. This is not a complete list but it does provide enough comparative information to show which troops, regiments or brigades suffered most severely in the battle. This is particularly revealing about the infantry brigades and shows that Charles Essex's brigade suffered more casualties cut down as they ran than Thomas Ballard's did fighting hard. The casualties in John Hamden's regiment suggest that his brigade may have fought with Royalist cavalry as it arrived during the closing stages of the battle.

	Warwick Accounts	Coventry accounts	Total casualties
Vantguard: Sir John Meldrum's Brigade			
Lord Saye and Sele's Regiment	8	1	9
Lord Robartes	0	2	2
Sir William Constable	25	2	27
Sir William Fairfax	6	1	7
Total			45
Battel: Charles Essex's Brigade			
Charles Essex's Regiment	22	6	28
Sir Henry Cholmley's Regiment	17	19	36
Lord Mandeville's Regiment	16	9	25
Lord Wharton's Regiment	13	7	20
Total			109
Rereguard: Thomas Ballard's Brigade			
The Lord General's Regiment	43	11	56
Lord Brooke's Regiment	11	2	13
Thomas Ballard's Regiment	1	2	3
Denzil Holles's Regiment	4	16	20
Total			92
John Brown's Dragoons	1	22	23
John Hamden's Regiment	7	0	7

Another record from Stratford-upon-Avon of 'monies disbursed and given unto Parliament soldiers which were wounded and died in the town after Kineton battle' includes 2 shillings and sixpence paid to George Popham, who was wounded serving under Captain Cromwell. This suggests that Captain Oliver Cromwell's troop suffered at least one casualty after it arrived during the closing stages of the battle.

Source: Dr E.E. Gruber von Arni Doctoral Thesis 'Who Cared – a study of the nursing cadre and welfare provided for soldiers and their families during the Civil War and Interregnum, 1642–1660 (Portsmouth University, 1999)

away, and on the enemy's side of those that stood; of whom I saw about threescore lie within the compass of threescore yards upon the ground whereon that brigade fought in which the King's standard was.'

Sir William Dugdale, the King's Rouge Croix Puirsuivant who was present during the battle, questioned local villagers who had buried corpses on the battlefield and he believed their count of around 1,000 to have been accurate. The wounded must have numbered between 2,000 or 3,000 more. Local villagers helped the wounded initially, some individuals making considerable efforts for their fellow Englishmen. Wounded Royalists were transported to Oxford and Parliamentarian wounded were concentrated at Coventry and Warwick. The Parliamentarian records are more detailed and demonstrate a greater degree of effort to assist their wounded men, both Lord Brooke and the Earl of Essex supplying funds for their care.

THE MARCH TO LONDON

By the third day after the battle some degree of order had returned to the King's army. The town of Banbury had been the immediate objective which had brought the two armies into conflict and the King was not about to lose the spoils of his claimed victory. The Royalist official account describes events: 'His Majesty the next Day drew out part of his Army, with some Ordnance, against the said Town; upon the approach of which the Rebels Forces (being the Earl of Peterborough's Regiment which were in the Town, to the number of 600) came out, laid down their Arms, and asked his Majesty Pardon; and immediately the Town was rendred up.'

The next day Prince Rupert proposed that he should ride with most of the Horse and Dragoons, reinforced by 3,000 commanded musketeers, to capture London. James II relates the outcome: 'But this so seasonable a proposition was first obstructed, and finally layd aside by the advice of many in the Councill, who were afraid least his Majesty shou'd return by conquest; one of them in plain terms telling him, that it was too hazardous for him to send Prince Rupert on that design, who being a young man, and naturally passionate might possibly be urg'd in heat of blood to fire the town.'

Instead the welcoming city of Oxford, offering a route to London only slightly circuitous but taking the Royalists out of striking range of Essex's line of march, proved too much of a temptation.

Essex wins the race to London

Marching from Warwick via Daventry and St Albans, Essex and his army were given a hero's welcome in London on 7 November. Parliament, moved by the King's proximity to London, despatched a petition offering a reconciliation and the King appeared ready to listen, suggesting Windsor castle as a location to conduct negotiations.

Essex's army began to deploy to cover the approaches to London. The Thames bridge at Kingston and the town of Brentford were to be guarded, the high ground around Acton garrisoned and Windsor Castle made a forward post. The Royalists interpreted these moves as attempts to entrap them as Bulstrode relates: 'News being then brought to the King, that Essex was advanced towards him, and had possessed the Passes of Windsor, Kingston and Acton, and that if Essex should also take Brentford, the King would be wholly surrounded, and deprived either of moving or subsisting.'

The battle for Brentford

On 11 November the Foot regiments of Lord Brookes and Denzil Holles, supported by a troop of Horse, arrived in Brentford, a small town on the banks of the Thames on the main road from the city to the west. The

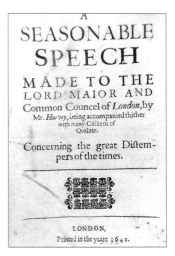

A speech by Edmund Harvey, a London merchant and Member of the Long Parliament, printed 27 December 1641. Harvey was a Captain in the White Regiment of the London Trained Bands at Turnham Green.

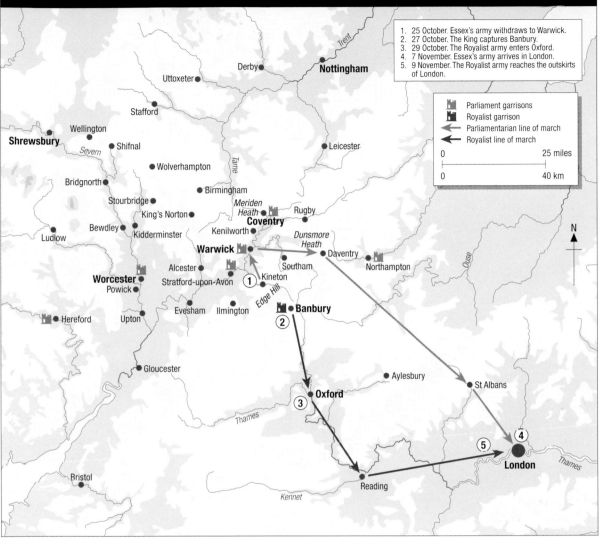

1. 25 October. Essex's army withdraws to Warwick.
2. 27 October. The King captures Banbury.
3. 29 October. The Royalist army enters Oxford.
4. 7 November. Essex's army arrives in London.
5. 9 November. The Royalist army reaches the outskirts of London.

Parliament garrisons	
Royalist garrison	
Parliamentarian line of march	
Royalist line of march	

0   25 miles
0   40 km

town was divided by a river, running into the Thames, into old and new Brentford. Holles's men established an outpost at the house of Sir Richard Wynne on the road running west to Hounslow, while the bulk of the regiment was drawn around the bridge linking the old and new town. Lord Brooke's Regiment established itself in the town and began to construct barricades. Given their hard service at Edgehill the two regiments taken together probably mustered about 1,000 men.

The Royalists decided to strengthen their position by capturing Brentford and opening the way to London: 'So the King marched with his whole army towards Brentford, where were two regiments of their best foot, (for so they were accounted, being those who had eminently behaved themselves at Edge-hill,) having barricadoed the narrow avenues to the town, and cast up some little breastworks at the most convenient places. Here a Welsh regiment of the king's, which had been faulty at Edge-hill, recovered its honour, and assaulted the works, and forced the barricadoes well defended by the enemy. Then the king's

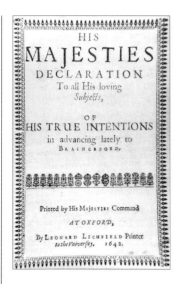

A Royalist account stating the King's intentions for his advance on Brentford.

forces entered the town after a very warm service, the chief officers and many soldiers of the other side being killed, and took there above five hundred prisoners, eleven colours, and fifteen pieces of cannon, and good store of ammunition.' [Clarendon]

The events of the battle of Brentford were as follows. On 12 November Parliament despatched Sir Peter Killigrew 'to know the King's pleasure concerning a cessation of arms during the time of this treaty', but when he reached Brentford he found the town under attack.

Under cover of a thick mist, Prince Rupert had attacked with some 2,000 Horse and Dragoons. After an initial rebuff Welsh infantry were called up in support and Holles's men were pushed back from their outpost at Sir Richard Wynne's house and then over the bridge to where Lord Brooke's men waited behind their barricades. A pamphlet entitled *A true and perfect relation of the barbarous and cruell passages of the king's army at old brainford*, published on 25 November 1642, alleges that the Royalists used prisoners as human shields: 'Even before the Fight begun at Old Brainford, with Colonell Hollis his Regiment, that they placed Ten of the Earl of Essex his souldiers (whom they had formerly taken prisoners at Keynton) pinioned, in the front of their men, to be as a Brestwork to receive the Bullets that came from Colonell Hollis his regiment, that the CAVALIERS might escape them, but such was the providence of God that not one of them was hurt, though shot through the clothes in many places.'

Bulstrode took part in the action and records the initial failure of Rupert's Horse to break into the town: 'The Prince of Wales's Regiment of Horse, where I was, being drawn up behind a great Hedge, where the Enemy had planted some Cannon, which we saw not, till they played so fast upon us, that we lost some Men, and were obliged to draw off and retire for our better Security; and upon our Foot's coming up, we beat the Regiments of Hambden and Hollis out of the Town, took several Prisoners and Arms, and sunk two great Barks in the River of Thames, with many Soldiers: And as two other Regiments came up to their Succour, they were also beaten, and we took some Colours and Cannon, and were intire Masters of Brentford.'

Officers of the London Trained Bands circa 1635. A good impression of the appearance of the Militia officers who served at Turnham Green.

The Royalist Foot regiment committed to the assault was that of Sir Thomas Salusbury. This was the Welsh regiment mentioned by Clarendon as recovering its honour at Brentford. John Gwynne, who served with the regiment, describes how the resolute defenders were surrounded on every side and then beaten out of the town to the river bank: 'We marched up to the enemy, engaged them by Sir Richard Winn's House, and the Thames side, beat them to retreat into Brainford, – beat them from the one Brainford to the other, and from thence to the open field, with a resolute and expeditious fighting, that after once firing suddenly to advance up to push of pikes and the butt-end of muskets, which proved so fatal to Holles his butchers and dyers that day, that abundance of them were killed and taken prisoners, besides those drowned in their attempt to escape by leaping into the river.' [*Military Memoirs of the Great Civil War*, London, 1822]

The fighting continued into the late afternoon when Hamden's Regiment arrived from its outpost at Uxbridge to cover the withdrawal of the survivors of Holles's and Brooke's regiments.

The pamphlet *A true and perfect relation of the barbarous and cruell passages of the king's army at old brainford* states that 10 of Holles' soldiers were killed and another 20 drowned, including Lieutenant-Colonel Jeremy Quareles and Captain Richard Lacey. Some 200 were captured, but at least 140 were released and rejoined the army, in the regiment of Sir Phillip Skippon as Holles's Regiment was not re-formed. It was alleged that the Royalists threatened their prisoners with hanging or being branded on the cheeks with hot irons if they refused to enlist in the King's army. The pamphlet goes on to tell of the atrocities in which the Royalists now indulged: 'They took after the fight ended, Five of the Earl of Essex his Souldiers, and tyed them by the hands with Ropes, and inforced them into the River of Thames, who standing in the water to their necks, casting their eyes on their Enemies, in hopes of Mercie; but such was the mercelesse condition of their Adversaries, that a Trooper rid into the water after them, and forced them to fall into the depth of the water, saying to them (in a jeering manner) Swim for your lives, when it was past all possibility to escape.'

Another account refers to the murder of wounded Parliamentarian soldiers by Royalist camp followers with their 'long knives'. The wide circulation of exaggerated accounts of these events helps to explain the growing antipathy of Parliamentarian soldiers to their Royalist opponents and helps to explain the mutilation of Royalist camp followers after the battle of Naseby.

Turnham Green

The events at Brentford gave form to all the fears that the citizens of London had been actively dwelling upon. The sacrifice of the regiments of Lord Brooke and Holles had given Essex time to bring his army together with the London Trained Bands out to Turnham Green, where they faced the King's army. It was obvious that all hope of an easy victory had again eluded the King. Even had his army succeeded in overcoming the great numerical superiority of Essex's forces it is likely that the Royalists would have suffered losses so great as to cripple their own army. With its citizens evidently hostile a pitched battle at the gates of London offered the King a poor prospect of a return to his capital. Ludlow

'Freeborn John' Lilburne. A political writer and pamphleteer before the Civil War and a leader in the Leveller movement after it. He served as a Captain in Lord Brooke's infantry regiment at Edgehill and was captured at Brentford.

Philip Skippon, Sergeant-Major General of the City of London and commander of the London Trained Bands at Turnham Green. Skippon was an experienced and highly competent professional soldier.

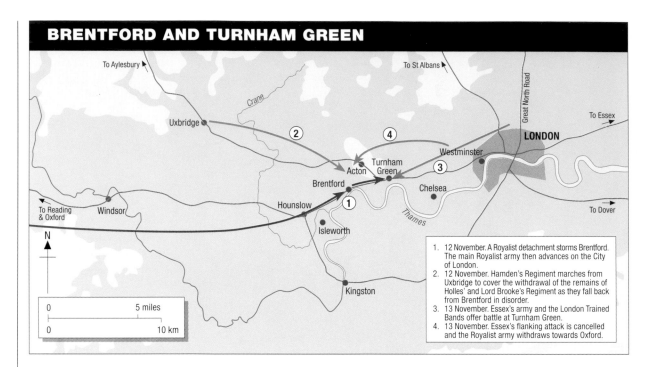

1. 12 November. A Royalist detachment storms Brentford. The main Royalist army then advances on the City of London.
2. 12 November. Hamden's Regiment marches from Uxbridge to cover the withdrawal of the remains of Holles' and Lord Brooke's Regiment as they fall back from Brentford in disorder.
3. 13 November. Essex's army and the London Trained Bands offer battle at Turnham Green.
4. 13 November. Essex's flanking attack is cancelled and the Royalist army withdraws towards Oxford.

describes how the Trained Bands rallied to the call of Parliament to defend their homes: 'By eight of the clock the next morning we had a body of twenty thousand horse and foot drawn up upon Turnham-green, a mile on this side of Brentford.'

Bulstrode Whitelocke, MP, recalls how Major-General Skippon led the London Trained Bands out of the city the following day encouraging 'his soldiers riding from one Company to another, & saying to them, Come my Boyes my brave Boyes, lett us pray heartily & fight heartily'. [*The Diary of Bulstrode Whitelocke 1605–1675* ed. Ruth Spalding 1990]

Whitelocke describes how the army was drawn up with its best Horse regiments in advance and the London Trained Band regiments interspersed amongst those of Essex's army: 'The whole Army was drawne up in Battalia in a Common called Turnham Green, their horse were strong, Sr Phillip Stapleton & Col Goodwyn with their Regiments had the Vanne, the other regiments of horse were placed in winges, the foote in the body one Regiment of the Citty & another of the Army next to one another.'

Essex ordered two regiments of Horse and four regiments of Foot to march out to Acton from where they might, at a pre-arranged signal, have fallen on the flank and rear of an attack by the King's army. This shows that Essex expected to fight that day, but as the Royalists showed no sign of intending to advance, the flanking force was recalled and the armies spent the day facing each other without coming to blows.

Bulstrode summed up the Royalists' reaction. Faced with the prospect of another major battle against fresh troops and overwhelming odds, and aware that the appearance of the London Trained Bands standing alongside Essex's army meant that the city was against them in spirit and in action 'finding the Earl of Essex, with his Army, was drawn out upon Turnham Green, with the Trained Bands of the City, and that the Enemy's Army was double to the King's, and that most of our

Ammunition was spent; it was therefore thought fit by the Council, that the King should retreat. Whereupon the King retired that Night to the Lord Cottington's House, near Hounslow, and we marched the next Day by Colebrook, towards Reading and Oxford, the first of which Places was garrisoned, and Oxford was the King's Head Quarters, where he made his Residence.'

The King withdraws

Far from recovering his capital and his Crown, the Edgehill campaign and the King's advance on London had driven the city into a closer and more determined support for Parliament and had forced its citizen soldiers of the London Trained Bands to take arms against him, opening the way for their active participation as part of Parliament's marching armies in the coming years.

With the year rapidly dwindling into short days and bad weather the Royalists turned to the happier prospect of a winter in loyal and welcoming Oxford. The chance for the King and Parliament to settle matters by a duel of their chosen armies had passed. Over the winter of 1642 the war would take on the characteristics of a prolonged national struggle during which every subject in the three kingdoms of King Charles would pay a price in treasure and blood.

VISITING THE BATTLEFIELD

Kineton can be reached by taking the B4451 from junction 12 of the M40. Turning on to the B4086 to Banbury, Edgehill will be seen as a low wooded ridge before and to the right of the road. Essex's positions are now occupied by a military depot, but one can reach the area in front of Radway where the Royalist army formed up.

From the top of Edgehill the ridge falls steeply some 350 feet to Radway, where rich farming land slopes gently down towards Kineton. A row of low buildings (the military storage bunkers) are visible in the middle distance marking the rising ground upon which Essex drew up his army. Many trees and woods are to be seen, but in 1642 trees were few and Edgehill itself was bare except for scrub bushes of the kind now seen only near Sun Rising.

The present patchwork of fields must be disregarded to visualise the armies drawn up in a great plain field or meadow, with smaller hedged enclosures on its flanks. The best, and most agreeable view of the battlefield is gained by following the B4086 up on to Edgehill and turning right to drive along the ridge to the Castle Inn. From the balcony of this welcoming establishment one obtains one of the most striking views offered by any English battlefield.

RIGHT **They are not forgotten. The Edgehill Memorial (on the B4086 Kineton to Banbury road) in early September 1999 shows that someone has remembered those who fought so long ago.**

OPPSITE **The Castle Inn seen from the base of Edgehill behind Radway village. This picture gives some idea of the steepness of the descent (falling 350 feet at this point) faced by the Royalist foot.**

BIBLIOGRAPHY

General Military Works

Barratt, J., 'Like an Iron Wall, New View of Royalist Cavalry Tactics'. *Military Illustrated* No. 96

Blackmore, D., *Arms & Armour of the English Civil Wars* (Royal Armouries, 1990)

Brzezinski, R., *The Army of Gustavus Adolphus, Infantry* (Osprey, MAA 235, 1991)

Brzezinski, R., *The Army of Gustavus Adolphus, Cavalry* (Osprey, MAA 262, 1993)

Brzezinski, R., *Lützen 1632 – Climax of the Thirty Years War* (Osprey, Campaign 68, 2001)

Elliott-Wright, Philip J.C., *Brassey's History of Uniforms, English Civil War* (London, 1997)

Firth, C.H., *Cromwell's Army* (Methuen, 1902)

Hutton, R., *The Royalist War Effort 1642-1646* (Longman, 1981)

Newman, P., *The Old Service, Royalist regimental colonels and the Civil War, 1642-46* (Manchester University Press, 1993)

Peachey, S., & Turton, A., *Old Robin's Foot, The equipping and campaigns of Essex's Infantry 1642-1645* (Partisan Press, 1987).

Reid, S., *All the King's Armies, A Military History of the English Civil War 1642-1651* (Spellmount, 1998)

Roberts, K., *Soldiers of the English Civil War (1) Infantry* (Osprey, Elite 25, 1989)

Roy, Dr I., *The Royalist Ordnance Papers 1642-1646 Parts I and II* (Oxfordshire Record Society, 1964 and 1978)

Tincey, J., *Soldiers of the English Civil War (2) Cavalry* (Osprey, Elite 27, 1990)

Turton, A., *The Chief Strength of the Army, Essex's Horse 1642-1645* (Partisan Press, 1992)

The Partisan Press series publishes a valuable range of books covering current military research on Civil War subjects.

Military Manuals

Barker, T.M., ed, *The Military Intellectual and Battle: Raimondo Montecuccoli and the Thirty Years War* (Albany, State University of New York Press, 1975)

Thomas Jenner, *The Military Discipline Wherein is Martially Showne the order for Driling the Musket and Pike* (London, 1642)

Alexander Leslie, Earl of Leven, *Generall Lessley's Direction and Order for the exercising of Horse and Foot* (London, 1642).

M.R., *A Compleat Schoole of Warre* (London, 1642)

John Raynsford, *The Young Soullder* (London, 1642)

Roberts, K., ed, Barriffe, *A Civil War Drill Book* (Partisan Press, 1988)

Young, P., ed, *Militarie Instructions for the Cavall'rie (being a facsimile of the edition of 1632 by John Cruso)* (The Roundwood Press, 1972)

The Battle of Edgehill

Bull, S., 'Artillery at Edgehill'. *Military Illustrated* No. 53

Davies, G., *The Battle of Edgehill* (EHR Vol 36, 1921)

Davies, G., *The Parliamentary army under the Earl of Essex 1642-1645* (EHR, 1934)

Peachey, S., ed, *The Edgehill Campaign & the letters of Nehemiah Wharton* (Partisan Press, 1989)

Roberts, K., 'Battle Plans' *English Civil War Times* No. 51

Sutton, J., *The Poets at War, a Verse-History of the Battle of Edgehill.* (Cromwelliana, 1992)

Tennant, P., *Edgehill and Beyond: The people's War in the South Midlands 1642-1645* (Stroud, 1992)

Young, P., *Edgehill 1642, The Campaign & the Battle* (The Roundwood Press, 1967)

Young, P., *King Charles I's Army of 1642* (JSAHR Vol 17, 1938)

Young, P., *The Royalist Artillery at Edgehill 23 October 1642* (JSAHR Vol 31, 1953)

Contemporary Newsbooks

The collection of the London bookseller George Thomason (c.1602-66) in the British Library is essential reading for any study of the Civil War. This consists of 22,255 pamphlets, newsbooks and manuscripts which Thomason collected between 1640 and 1663. The collection includes 1,966 pamphlets and 167 newsbooks printed in 1642.

INDEX

COMPANION SERIES FROM OSPREY

MEN-AT-ARMS

An unrivalled source of information on the organisation, uniforms and equipment of the world's fighting men, past and present. The series covers hundreds of subjects spanning 5,000 years of history. Each 48-page book includes concise texts packed with specific information, some 40 photos, maps and diagrams, and eight colour plates of uniformed figures.

ELITE

Detailed information on the uniforms and insignia of the world's most famous military forces. Each 64-page book contains some 50 photographs and diagrams, and 12 pages of full-colour artwork.

NEW VANGUARD

Comprehensive histories of the design, development and operational use of the world's armoured vehicles and artillery. Each 48-page book contains eight pages of full-colour artwork including a detailed cutaway.

WARRIOR

Definitive analysis of the armour, weapons, tactics and motivation of the fighting men of history. Each 64-page book contains cutaways and exploded artwork of the warrior's weapons and armour.

ORDER OF BATTLE

The most detailed information ever published on the units which fought history's great battles. Each 96-page book contains comprehensive organisation diagrams supported by ultra-detailed colour maps. Each title also includes a large fold-out base map.

AIRCRAFT OF THE ACES

Focuses exclusively on the elite pilots of major air campaigns, and includes unique interviews with surviving aces sourced specifically for each volume. Each 96-page volume contains up to 40 specially commissioned artworks, unit listings, new scale plans and the best archival photography available.

COMBAT AIRCRAFT

Technical information from the world's leading aviation writers on the aircraft types flown. Each 96-page volume contains up to 40 specially commissioned artworks, unit listings, new scale plans and the best archival photography available.